BOY OF
"GREATEST"

DAVID W. LAWRIE

Heritage Special Edition
American Literary Press

Baltimore, Maryland

Boy of "Greatest"

Library of Congress
Cataloging-in-Publication Data
ISBN-13: 978-1-934696-17-0

Library of Congress Card Catalog Number:
2008929321

Published by

Heritage Special Edition
American Literary Press

8019 Belair Road, Suite 10
Baltimore, Maryland 21236

Manufactured in the United States of America

I dedicate the following pages to any future "boy" as a beginner's map to "manhood."

REMEMBER

It was the Veteran, not the reporter,
Who has given us freedom of the press.

It was the Veteran, not the poet,
Who has given us freedom of speech.

It was the Veteran, not the lawyer,
Who has given us the right to a fair trial.

It was the Veteran, not the campus organizer,
Who has given us the right to demonstrate.

It was the Veteran who salutes the flag,
Who served under the flag,
Whose coffin is draped by the flag,
Who allows the protester to burn the flag.

Father Dennis O'Brien, USMC

Above: *Big Hands Embrace Parents*. Last visit home before deployment, 1942.

Left: David Lawrie (on right), age eleven, with first cousin David Laverty, KIA 1941 … I enlisted for vengeance.

I

Opening Statement: Salt Lake City, 5/05/07
VIRGINS ALL

I'm writing this at the request of my friends and neighbors. Since my wife has long ago passed on and relatives live far away, these neighbors of mine care for me, as I have cared for their children, even as many of the children have grown—college kids who, like their parents, still visit me and give such a boost to my morale, with a hug or a peck on the cheek. That's my good side, helping kids grow; not as enclosed—my eventual shooting of others, and not just shooting them, but doing it with triumph, putting them down. . . . To the moms with their love and care and the dads with their physical support, I dedicate this true story, with no "filling" added, the memory of my sojourn, with many, many other guys, fellow Americans. It's sometimes funny, sometimes not, my time as a First Infantry Division rifleman, first squad, first platoon, Company A, twenty-sixth infantry regiment, "Big Red One," "Private" A.S.N. 12065322.

Since the neighbors have visited me at the VA hospital various times, they know I'm a "disabled veteran of WWII," soon to be a rare breed. I must add many thanks to the VA hospitals, with all their cutting and patching to keep me alive, the care and visual pleasure of the spotless whites and proud peaked hats of the lovely nurses I owe so much to. Unfortunately, nurses today are required to dress like janitors, to be "politically correct." This denies patients the balm of seeing the sight of a comforting woman in white, dispensing love and care, same as it would come from a mother or sister. I'm knocking eighty-five and can't go skiing or chase girls, not even the old ones anymore. I tire easily. It suits me to sit here almost like in meditation and use my pencil as a magic wand to take a trip, or a ride along

1

a path long forgotten, sometimes smooth, sometimes rough, very rough. And as I write and as I concentrate I feel my pencil is like a probe lifting the edge of a rug, an opaque rug, the rug I had spread over my memory.

The things, real things, that happened to me over sixty-five years ago, things I'm sure I would never have thought of again, because they belong to someone else, someone who for long years I tried to forget. But now in my eighties, close to my end of track, who cares? Let it out, ALL of it. Let's hear from him again. My prying pencil excites a dead or long-covered part of my mind, the part that knows, knows absolutely, that this is no made-up story, no make-believe, no effort to praise myself. That would be impossible, as too many other men were with me. Stood with me. Held my life in their hands, as I held theirs. Even the men who worked in the rear, doing a job, keeping the food, ammunition, handling the equipment the fighting guys needed. They stood the chance of being killed or wounded, and often were. I couldn't possibly praise myself. Believe me, everyone was, accidentally or not, a hero. Either standing tall or disintegrating under pressure.

Now, this is not primarily about the war as such; that's the background. This is about a single solider, a "private" all the way, and the impressive high points that stuck to his retentive mind. And only that. No embellishments. It's not about a lot of heroics, although there's some, or about killing, although there's some. No dipping into the depth's of fear and despair, although there's some. And although of course I never thought about it at the time (never kept any notes), this could be a means to clue in others who have ever wondered what goes on in the mind of a young man, off on the supposedly innocent excitement of wanting to be a soldier, a real "soldier," a fighting soldier able in time to stand shoulder to shoulder with all the proud patriotic men of his country since its inception. Like in all the books he has read or movies he's seen in his boyhood, it's true that a soldier eventually has to be hard and kill people, whereas a doctor is nice and heals people. But both are necessary. I give you, you might say, a glimmering into a distant memory, to follow an eventual soldier through his violent baptism, wrung from a peacetime boyhood, to an epitome of hell. But the violence, the fear, the determination to do his duty, coming together in his young mind to eventually produce what he wished to be, a soldier. Here is this soldier's story, less the *F* word. I despise brainless, false verbal courage. I live by a "don't say it if you can't do it" attitude.

Since the U.S. Army doesn't award medals to men for killing the enemy, but does give them an award for being killed or wounded by them, I have only to "so to speak" the ones I earned, because the Germans never did tag me, despite their many, many tries. They never did manage to ring the bell, although I rang theirs. "Ding-dong, ding-dong." What did get me, however, was the blast of a stack of 75-mm shells exploding, no doubt from rough handling by Italian PWs (prisoners) after delivering a truckload of approximately two hundred shells, and watching these people rolling them and stacking them, CRASH, BANG. I had parked down at the end of a line of six-by-sixes (trucks) and I walked back to bull a little with the POW guard. I asked if it wasn't dangerous banging shells around like that. He said not to worry, they couldn't go off without a fuse. Now that sounds reasonable, but it also sounds like "famous last words." Another driver standing next to me said he was going to write home, and I thought this was a good chance for me to do it too, and walked back to the truck. It was a six-by-six with an open cab; that is, one that has no doors, roof or back, only a windshield. I remember putting a writing pad on the steering wheel and starting, "Dear Mom," and the next thing, or the first thing, of consciousness I can remember after that in the fuzz of my mind was that I was climbing a wall, or trying to. I had to get away. I was clawing up this wall trying to get away but something heavy was on my back. Somehow I couldn't reach the top. And I could hear a howling sound of wind rushing through my head; must be the breath of something bad coming at me. Christ! A Dragon! The Dragon I had both feared and revered has finally crushed me! That must be it; it's got me! Let me goooo!

Faces were looking at me; the faces were wearing American helmets. That calmed me. Christ, fellows, help me! Help me get over this wall, then I'll be okay! Then I felt hands lifting and pulling on me.

I had been just far enough away from the blast that it didn't kill me, and the lack of a truck cab let me be blown out, no doubt saving me from being crushed inside of it. Also, the fact that my head was bent over the note pad saved me from the flash burn. I was told later that the only other driver to survive besides myself had been badly burned on his side. They found me still clawing at the ground, the ground that I had imagined was a wall, and gravity was the weight pressing me down against the "wall." The howling in my head and ears stayed with me for, I don't know, a month or more.

My injuries and memories can't possibly be in chronological order. I still feel some things are missing, but I'll try. One thing I still see is the khaki wall of a tent in the 77th Evacuation Hospital and the incredibly soft hands and smile of an American nurse. I knew she was an American because she was beautiful, and I could see her eyes were glistening for me, like a mother crying over a child. And bit by bit in time this is where many of these memories came back to me. I really shouldn't say "memories," its more like me, David Lawrie, slowly having my brains start connecting again, telling me who I was, and where I was, and what was I doing!

No doubt the steering wheel is what caused my severe internal injuries; my stomach and other organs were crushed up under my rib cage, causing in time the replacement of my stomach with an intestine. This has worked fine, except I have no valve at the top. I must be careful not to overeat or drink fluid too fast, or I get terrible heart burn and my body gets clammy. My right leg was badly twisted and I suffered in time a very painful recovery from a surgery on my knee. But unfortunately it would not work; eventually, the entire knee had to be removed and replaced with a metal one. Five fractures were found in my spine, where muscles that were attached to the spine and bone from my hip were used to "fuse" them. Again this works, but I can't completely bend over, or when lying down I must first turn over on my side to rise. Also, my left eye was blown in in a way that caused the retina to collapse, leaving me blind in that eye, which meant, of course, I was only one eye away from being totally blind. Not a pleasant thought! Having no lasers then, the eye was taken out, cut open, and the retina was stitched back in place. I was warned not to expect a miracle, but I got one! The eye has what they call a "buckle;" the eyeball is now shaped like a pear. If I lift the eyelid it can be seen. Weird but working. I lost the ability to read lying down because the odd shape of the eyeball causes irritation, but who cares about that!

I can see 20/40. The doctors said it was exceptional, but to me it was my "miracle." How about that!

In time my gallbladder and appendix had to be removed, and now just lately I have been given a quadruple heart bypass. I also came home with colitis, amebic dysentery and malaria. I drank the water instead of the "vino." All this but no Purple Heart because they say injuries must be caused by enemy action, not by stupid mishandling of shells! All of this is a matter of record. Remember my promise . . . to tell only what I know to be true. Or would you like me to lift my eyelid? Oh yeah!

Today in the halls of the VA hospital I see what's left of all the fine young men I served with; they're reduced to rubble, in the wreckage of what's called "old age." My mind rebels. That can't be me. I can't look like one of them! I'm still only twenty-years old, if I just don't look in a mirror. Oh yeah . . . to think we were once the best! The tip of the country's spear! Now, instead of admiration, we receive sympathy. "Hey, grandpa! You did real good! Hang on! Oh yeah!

The government has held to its pledge that all combat veterans of this or any future war will receive the best of care. I've been cut up, sewed up, and cared for in the best-equipped hospitals by teams of doctors and nurses for sixty years now. I'm sure money couldn't buy better. My official disability rating is 70 percent, which means, of course, as my wife used to say, I get all my operations for free. My rejoinder, and I must always have a rejoinder: Yes, honey, I'm sure that ranks up there with getting free hemorrhoids!

I understand in WWII fifteen million men and women at one time or another served our country. I'm sure everyone had a beginning. Since some 400,000 didn't make it back, that would still be fourteen million plus who could write about their first days in the service. Now, here is one—mine.

My generation was born in the twenties, the "roaring twenties." Unfortunately, the bubble burst in 1929. I was seven years old, and the rest of growing up was in the "Great Depression." It wasn't so bad for the youth, because you can't miss what you never had. But things were "tight," no faking it. School was strict. Jobs for grown men were hard to come by, and what money there was, was real, backed by silver or gold. Not the "Monopoly" money that we pay baby-sitters seven dollars an hour with today. But the best for me was the birth of a tough Manhattan kid in 1920 who was to become my assigned "brother," my brother in arms; we were to live as close as "Siamese." My absolute duty was to cover his back, as his was to cover mine. One never to fail the other. So help us God! Rich stuff for a couple of "Boy Scouts." His name was "Solan," my designated "buddy," and eventually he both lent me strength and multiple time's saved my life.

Now, here's about my induction . . . induction to the U.S. Army, that is . . .

Big things always start small. It was a Sunday afternoon in December 1941. I was nineteen. Nineteen! Now there's a thought. Nineteen, I was in my prime, on the verge of manhood. Growing up I could always remember playing in empty lots, all of them hadn't been filled with apartment houses yet, or we could play in the streets, hand ball or stick ball. I could hit two "sewers." One sewer was always home plate, the next was second, in between a car's fender was either first or third, if one was there; cars hadn't yet filled every block from avenue to avenue. You could ride on a trolley for a nickel, or for free if you hung on the back. Of course, you had to watch out that some tough Irish cop didn't see you and give you a not-too-gentle rap across your butt with his inevitable "nightstick." No "lasers" then, just muscle power. The radio had just been invented and the masses were just beginning to hear canned music.

Us kids on a Saturday would get our pennies together and go to a United cigar store, where they sold large five-cent candy bars, three for ten cents, then go to a movie for another dime and watch the cowboy save the sweet, innocent heroine from the dastardly Indian. Unashamed we cheered. Yeah! Another dead Indian. Can you believe it? We were not yet "politically correct."

In the schools a teacher could use a ruler to rap your hand or maybe a knuckle to tap the back of your head. Ouch! I got that more than once. No one was fat. McDonald's hadn't been invented yet, and your mother had to feed you breakfast and give you a sandwich and a piece of fruit for lunch to take to school. We didn't have soda machines; we had water fountains, and you could drink all you wanted. In those days, mothers, God bless them, stayed home so that any child knew home meant love and care, love and safety in the arms of "Mom," who was always there. And every "Mom" gave her all, unstintingly.

Winter in Brooklyn was always a ball after the snow, usually a foot at a time. Snow plows would come down the street mounted on big old WWI trucks. These trucks had big, solid rubber tires and no drive shaft. They ran by using chains on the rear wheels, and the uncovered, visible, very visible chain drive grinding and roaring was enough to warn, "stay away!" Big ugly trucks with there huge, flat, solid rubber tires commanded the street. The joke was that if ever one of them ran over anybody, you could take him home, and if no one was home, just slide him under the door. Har! Har! The plows would leave big heaps of snow on one side of the street, where we could slide up and down or make forts inside. If we had more snow, then this time the plows would fill the other side, giving us a chance to have snowball fights between forts.

Inevitably our bodies grow, responding to our built-in program, that insidious program that causes us all to be what we are, first boys or girls, then men or women, then, finally, working up to mothers or providers, and finally, "groan," grandparents. The program we all carry inside of us begins to signal (to me anyway), "Girls, girls? Sure! They're not so bad; in fact, they are kind of nice. Go ahead, act silly, maybe you can attract one." And if you do, and begin to enjoy female company, you take her out to a movie. It will only cost fifty cents—fifteen cents each to get in, and ten cents each for an ice cream sundae afterwards. Who knows, you might wind up liking it, like your still-unknown internal program wants you to! Nature is sneaky.

I was immersed in a dream, a dream far from Brooklyn. I remember this night because it was one of the few times I got to talk to Solan like just a pal, not a buddy, but a friend. You might not follow me, but a friend is like an old pal. Pals come and go, but a buddy is far more than that. In the army, in wartime, a buddy, I would say to give a proper description, is like a part of yourself. Like conjoined

7

twins, inseparable, incapable of one ever leaving the other, no matter what might rain down. I was huddled in our foxhole hugging my "piece," as always. My piece (rifle) was always fully loaded, safety on. It not only gave me comfort smelling it, but the innate supreme power of it in my arm. I could sleep fearless, my buddy having the watch. I had a blanket pulled over my head. I liked it like that, shutting out the world. The world that had changed so fearsomely. As I said, I was dreaming, and I often remember this because now, today, safe at home, the dream is the opposite. I can't believe that all the hell and destruction I knew wasn't something I had read in a book. Then I felt the pressure of a hand and its hold on my arm. Pressing the arm, leg, whatever, then holding it was the only way to wake anyone. The press was to wake you, and the holding was to signal all was okay. Take it easy, it's just your time to wake up, which was usually to stand guard. If you shouted at a guy or roused him by a poke or pull you might catch a bullet! It was only Solan with quiet insistence, just above a whisper, "Dave, Dave."

I didn't wake up grumpy this time. My mind was slow to let go of the pleasure of the dream. I have said before, I can't remember things exactly or words that were spoken, and I won't fill in by making up something, but this night and these words I remember well because I thought of them so often. I said, "Jeez, Solan, I was dreaming, playing ball, chasing girls, the good food, Hershey Bars and Cokes that we had at home. Did that really happen, or was it something we read in a book?"

"No, Dave," he mused. His face seemed to go soft. "Yeah, that was real. That was the time—the gaudy lights, the traffic, and the Paramount theater with all the big bands. We could make the balcony jump as we yelled and kept time." His face seemed too close up again. "Bet on it, Dave. That was real, and I miss it too, but we'll get it back. We'll get it back, once we smear all these bastards. Now get up, and don't be dreaming on watch!"

Sorry I wandered off again, so far from my induction. My pencil surely took me on a premature ride down memory again. How about we get back?

I was nineteen and the Japanese had just bombed Pearl Harbor.

I was with a pal of mine at a local park, watching small kids play baseball, when we decided to have some lunch at a local lunch wagon we lovingly called "the roach coach." No fast-fatting food places then. The owner had the radio on (no TV then) and he was saying, "Listen, boys! Listen! The Japs have just bombed Pearl Harbor!" And everyone was asking, "Where's Pearl Harbor?" Then it came out that it was in Hawaii. Some beach in Hawaii? Why would they do that? No one knew at the time that the navy had put all of its eggs in this tiny basket, a small harbor, so small ships had to be moored together; men on the outboard ships had to go ashore by climbing over the inboard ones. They said the Jap bombers were the best! Best!? With all the ships moored together, they couldn't miss! Like shooting fish in a barrel.

I felt the same as every other American felt. The Japanese had to be crazy! California alone was bigger than Japan. We would surely pay them back. And no slant-eye would be left to kill anymore of our people. Only four months later my family was informed that my close cousin, David Laverty, my mother's brother's son, had been killed in the Philippines. He had been a soldier. So at nineteen, I went and enlisted; I didn't wait to be drafted. I wanted to make good for him, to get away from home, to become the great avenging "Jap killer," and also have the great adventure! So on June 12, 1942, I became number 12065322 in the U.S. Army, joining the ranks of the thousands of men who were fighting or who had fought for our great country.

I reported to Grand Central Station, along with many other guys, and boarded a train that took us to Fort Dix, New Jersey. When we got to Fort Dix, we were assigned to different areas to clean or "police," as it was called. A lot of guys complained about not getting uniforms, but others wisely said, "Once we get in them, you may never get out of them." And true enough, many were buried in them. Oh yeah!

Well, we got our uniforms, and at least we looked organized, but no helmets. We had all heard about the new helmets but there weren't any. Later—if it wasn't something left over from WWI we had to wait. We were all given shots, and it's not true that some guys fainted from the needle. It wasn't the needle, it was what was in the needle. Some shots felt like being hit with a hammer. Ouch! No, I'm not the fainting kind!

We passed through like a big barn filled with rows and rows of clerks with typewriters, all going a mile a minute, taking down pertinent information from each man and also, as I was to remember later, filling out a form for life insurance, ten thousand dollars each. If you got killed, your mom and dad would get it. And here my first weird trick in the army would occur. It wasn't until I was in a hospital in England that I found out my rapidly typing clerk had left off a zero. I had been through eight months of combat, with only one thousand dollars for my parents. And that doesn't include eight months of training in the U.S., where more than a few guys were killed or died from the exertion, from May 1942 to December 1942. Then in January 1943 I joined the First Infantry Division overseas, starting two months of combat time with a rifle (the hairiest), then six months with the regimental ammunition officer (hair, but not standing), through to the finish of Africa and the invasion and occupation of Sicily, until August 1943. That finished my eight months of combat time. The rest was hospital time, eleven months.

When I told my Dad this, he laughed. Said it was good. That's why the Buggers didn't kill me, I wasn't worth it! Better still, when I applied for the missing nine thousand dollars I was refused. The reason given—I was in unfit condition!

In September 1943 I left First Division, was hospitalized in Sicily, England, and U.S. for eleven months, and was honorably discharged in July 1944—twenty-seven months of service altogether. I'm not complaining, just compiling. Have I compiled enough?

LISTEN, LET'S RECOUNT. HOW MANY MEN HAVE LIVED THROUGH THE SOARING HEIGHTS AND FEARFUL, MIND-BLOWING DEPTHS AS MEN LIKE MYSELF, WHO HAVE ENDURED AND ENJOYED THE RIDE, THE FEARFUL RIDE ON THE DRAGONS BACK—MAXIMUM ADRENALINE!— THEN ESCAPED THE FIERY BREATH AND THE TEARING, BLOODY CLAWS AMID THE BODIES AND BONES OF SO MANY OTHERS? YOU WANT SOMETHING BETTER THAN SEX?! ENLIST! OH YEAH!

Back to Fort Dix. I'll never forget my first night in the army. We were all issued mattress covers and told to fill them with straw to sleep on. We didn't know it then, but these covers were also just the right size to hold a body for burial. There were no plastic bags then, and in the action to come, many times you would see these bags with some guy's legs sticking out with the bottom of the bag tied to them. The feet would only have socks on them, as shoes and boots were always saved to recycle. Seeing this, many of the guys would crack how someone had won the royal order of the "mattress cover." Oh yeah! I wasn't aware of this at the time, and stuffed mine with straw and lay down to sleep.

It was some kind of a big, gloomy barn, dark, filled with snoring, wheezing, men breaking wind, grunting and smelling like wet socks. Jeez! I thought, *What have I done?!* I had to enlist! What a nut! Finally, with the help of an exhausting day I fell asleep. The next day, to be my first full day in the army, we were marched off to a mess hall for breakfast. They didn't use trays then. Everything was eaten off a plate or bowl. As we moved along a line, I picked up a bowl, and then a guy, one of the long-time soldiers, plopped a big helping of oatmeal into it. I thought, *Great!* I was brought up on oatmeal. But before I could move along, the next "old time," "real soldier" serving the food (you could always tell these guys because they always wore a "smoky" flat hat to show they weren't crummy recruits) dropped a full ladle of sugar on my oatmeal. I shoved it back! I didn't want sugar.

He said, "Well, you've got it now; move along."

I said, "Aw, come on, don't be dumb; give me a bowl without sugar!"

This time with a curved lip he grumbled with menace, "Move along or I'll shove it up your ass."

What?! You will!? Now, I'm usually never at a loss for words. Looking up, my eyes lit on his hat—symbol of authority, the Holy Grail of the "real" soldiers. What a chance! I said, "Oh yeah! And I'll piss in your hat!" Bull's-eye.

He looked stunned, but not for long. Over he came. Over the counter, benches, dishes, silverware. Oh, Mother! A crumb of a recruit to answer back! Like hell you will. Curses changed to grunts as I pummeled a tune on his ribs until some officer yelled, "ATTENTION!" (That's an officer's call to STOP whatever you're doing.) Could be a general might be coming. Then, just like in the movies, my first day was spent on KP picking eyes out of potatoes, washing dishes and being threatened by the mess sergeant with a firing squad if I caused any more trouble! Oh yeah! Just getting acquainted.

Fort Dix was a reception center. This is where the clerk managed to put me down for a thousand dollars of insurance instead of ten thousand. Just the first hint of the many odd things that would both fall on me (ugh!) sometimes and then again magically, like a gift from the Gods, pull my desperate ass out of a hole when I believed my ass was gonna be gone. And later, after "Kasserine," the bitter memory of being read the "Articles of War," how you could be shot for desertion or failing to fight. Remembering this is what made me so mad when I thought our army, the U.S. Army, had run off and left me and Solan and my company, Company "A" 26th infantry, first battalion, without ammunition, to be overrun by the 21st Panzer Division. We had no chance! Some of us got away, and then even so we damn sure didn't leave peacefully! In this case it wasn't *us* that ran off. It was the U.S. Army! What article of war covers that? Neither they nor we will ever forget "Kasserine Pass," and if you check your history books, we took the pass back soon enough, and the Germans never stopped running until they surrendered Africa. Oh yeah!

Note: In 2004 I read in a book, *An Army At Dawn*, that two attempts to reach Company "A" with needed supplies in "Kasserine" were beaten off by the Germans. I'm happy; it really made me feel ashamed of my accusation! We hadn't been deserted. We had even lost men trying to get to us.

Well, the pencil has done it again. Can't seem to stay on the subject. To get back, since I had enlisted and had not been drafted, I was allowed to choose my branch of service. I chose the Armored Force, and in time I was sent to Fort Knox for training. We were glad to arrive in Kentucky, away from all the stenches of the slaughter houses of pigs, cows, horses, whatever, all along the tracks through New Jersey until we got there.

Fort Knox, Kentucky, blue grass and fresh air. And there they were! Tanks. Look at them! Big, huge machines. Imagine what I can do in one of them! Look at the size of the cannons and multiple machine guns sticking out! In time I was to learn these were Grant Tanks, and if these weren't powerful enough, there were soon to be even newer Sherman Tanks. We were to learn all about the various tanks in our ten weeks of training. We were shown films of the Germans and their army marching around to a snare drum; just shoot the officer or the sergeant and the rest will surrender. Oh yeah! It showed that all they ever had to fight with were those crappy little two-man tanks, and the Japanese had much the same. Our Shermans would demolish them. Hell, we couldn't wait to get started as tank operators. But believe me, you couldn't be just a driver, you had to be an operator. Decompressing the radial engine fifty times, then using a shotgun shell to start, praying that it would, or you would have to do the routine again. Learn Morse code—no voice transmitting then. The care of the 37-mm cannon, 50-cal machine gun, strip and clean, and 30-cal machine guns.

And then for the great reward we all hungered for. On some mornings we would be marched out in our new indestructible shoes some five miles. The morning walk included what was fittingly called "Agony Hill" to the training area, and there designated drivers would take turns learning to drive a tank, the real thing, with others over an obstacle course. Man, what power! Bring on those Dragons. You could feel the power running up your arms as you controlled it. Sounds easy, but nothing in the army is made easy. It's called toughening up and training. First, fall in with filled canteens. The canteen must last you for the day; this is called canteen training. After our hike when we arrived at the training area, sweated up and panting, we would be given a sandwich of jelly and peanut butter, well heated by the Kentucky sun to make it stick to the roof of your mouth. That would be unpleasant food training. Ugh! Then, after more instruction of the inside of the tank, we'd get the chance alternately to drive the monster, and to us it was a monster. Twelve tons of steel and a cannon. A 37-mm cannon.

Now, of course if any of us had known the Germans already had tanks up to *seventy tons* and a cannon of *88-mm*, enough to blow us away from a mile away (and that's no exaggeration) before we could even scratch their paint, we'd have all run off and hidden in the woods. But being ignorant young men (oh, I don't like the word "ignorant;" let's just call them "virgins"), we all trained to be the formidable foe of the Japanese or possibly the Germans, who we were shown conquering the French with their tiny two-man peanut tanks.

Then, worst of all, the knuckle-busting job of replacing a thrown track, which I would imagine is a heart-stopper to do in combat. We were told that if ever we were "immobilized" we should stay inside the tank and become a "metal pillbox." But of course the people training us really knew no more than we did. In truth, any tank stopping in combat would immediately draw fire from every enemy weapon until it blazed up or blew up. Elementary! A stationary target is much easier to hit than a moving one. Even though you stood a poor chance of jumping out, if you didn't, your death would be certain!

Well, anyway, that was in the future. Right now we had table work, stripping machine guns, hand guns and 45-cal Thomsons. Training on the 37-mm cannon was done with an adapter firing 22-cal bullets—at that time the U.S. Army didn't have enough 37s on hand! All of this was taught to us by "real" soldiers, them being allowed to wear their "smoky hats" to show they were above the new flood of recruits. I shouldn't be hard on them. They were mainly middle-aged soldiers, or some kind of losers; they were in the army because of the depression. These "real" soldiers did their best, and of course they delighted in little harassments. Remember, soldier, "yous always got a choice. Yous gotta do what you're told, but yous don't gotta like it." Har! Har! Oh yeah!

Believe it or not, when war was declared the U.S. Army amounted to less than the army of Portugal. God bless politicians! Or is it the other way around? The Japanese admitted that our lack of a real standing armed force encouraged them to attack.

Well, to get back to Fort Knox. Again a little argument. Shirts off. I got my lumps; wasn't too bad as I got to give some back. These "regulars" might be dumb, in their perverse attitude of acting tough, or maybe they weren't acting. I would certainly agree there are no cream puffs among them. It could be my Scotch-American genes' perverse attitude that takes offense and gets me to punching and in trouble, or it could be the result of all those "shots" and horsehide shoes we had to break in (ow!) crippling my niceness, making me want to beat on someone. But us recruits were warned in time, cool it, or no weekend passes.

Now, weekend passes were like coming up for a breath of non-army air. No one wanted to loose them. And the army has ways. Foul up, and your entire squad shares the demerits too. And things, I believe you could say, will get unpleasant for the malefactor.

Now here's a pleasant/unpleasant weekend I shared with a friend from Brooklyn . . .

I had altered my New York driver's license to show that I was twenty-two, not nineteen. You had to be twenty-one to rent a car in Louisville, Kentucky. My friend from Brooklyn was with me.

We had both gone to P.S. 170 as boys. It was a school five stories high. And as you progressed, you climbed more stairs. One day, running in the hall to get to my class, as I rounded a corner I came forehead to forehead with another boy and all the lights went out. Next I saw a teacher's face from the prone position I was in, babbling away as she dripped water on my face. For the first time ever I had been knocked unconscious, and I guess my mind has been addled ever since. Hey, David, watch it! Where would you be without me, your ever loving mind?

Speaking about being unconscious, where was I? Oh yeah, speaking about the guy from Brooklyn. Somehow, having been among so many strange and unfamiliar other guys from different states, it was a pleasure to buddy up with someone from home. And we both wanted to get a break from the men, men, men; we wanted to get around some girls. So, what better way? We went in style, renting a car.

After scouting around in Louisville for awhile without any luck, we wound up over in Jefferson, Indiana (across the river), where there was a USO that had a room full of teenage girls. After a little dancing and sodas, we sneakily arranged to meet two of them outside. Rules said they weren't allowed to leave with "guests." Oh, ho!

We got this couple to take a ride with us, and did some real heavy petting, more than we were ever allowed by the girls at home. These Southern girls were more passionate; it was more hands, and mouths, and touching, but even by using that old worn-out cliche, "We are soldiers off to war and may soon die," we struck out. Nope, no sale. Pushed away. No penis tonight, boys, put them away. Hell, I wouldn't have known what to do with it anyway. The full extent of its nature had never been used. None of us had the experience. So with fond farewells, we took them home.

We were given a rain check for the following week, but all wasn't lost sexually; we did get a step up the ladder, so to speak, suffering for the first time from what the army had warned us about: "lover's nuts." Sounds funny, but it's very pain full. After we took the two teasers home we checked into a crummy hotel back in Louisville. Real upscale. Oh yeah! It had marks of the height of the most recent flood proudly enshrined on the wall. What a dump. Who cares? We both lay on the beds moaning and holding ourselves, wondering if the aching would be permanent because we had been warned about such things in our indoctrination. We had already checked ourselves and were happy to see that they (our pride and joy) hadn't turned blue. At least not yet. Oh, Mother! Oh yeah! Those girls really taught us what the word "tease" means. But I'll bet if those girls are still alive today, even though they must be old grandmothers, they still remember the feel of those two Yankee boys they got hold of. Oh yeah!

Now to continue. The day I left Fort Knox to go back to Fort Dix to make ready for embarkation (overseas) the sergeant I had the tussle with seemed affable enough. He gave me a slight "hi" sign and I thought he was okay. He hadn't gotten back at me with dirty details or whatever, a good old Joe. Must have been about thirty or so, but again no cream puff; he had given me a split inner cheek. I hate that; makes it hard to eat, especially anything hot. But I bet he still felt the pummeling I had given him on his ribs; guess I made him groan a bit. Waving goodbye, he surely had the last laugh, as I found out when I got to Africa. Did I say dumb? He changed my entire life with the use of one word. He changed my designation as a replacement from First <u>Armored</u> Division to First <u>Infantry</u> Division! Touché, up yours, or whatever that means . . .

Well, to get back, if you can still follow me. A real old man, a conductor was hollering at me. Alright, alright, soldier boy, if you're going, get aboard! Yes, sir. I climbed onto a big day coach filled with noisy, rambunctious young men; you would think we were going to a party. All the shades were drawn and we were not allowed to raise them. That was, I guess, to keep any spies from seeing it was full of kid soldiers going off to war. No one had told us where we were going, but as we picked up speed I could see the sun was on our left. Hey, hey, that ain't the way to the Pacific! We're going back east. And we did; we went back to Fort Dix. This time as our port of embarkation.

I drew all my equipment, including those long-awaited new helmets, and then got one last pass to go home. This time I hitched a ride to get to a ferry in Jersey that would get me over to Manhattan and from there a subway to Brooklyn. The car I hitched a ride in was a brand new 1941 Chevrolet. Amazingly it was already all battered up. The two old coots singing and laughing in it offered men a shot of old "Pecker Head," good for snake bites and delirium tremors. Even showed me the snake head in the bottle, Great Christ! I said, "No, thanks, I'm going to visit my parents." It dawned on me that these two were moonshiners and no doubt their driving the back roads of Jersey to get to and from their still was what caused the nice new car to be in such a battered condition. But they got me to the ferry. That's all that mattered, because this was the visit my dad explained about "Buggers" and that to steady my mind I should always think of "getting" and not of being "got." It was the thought that always stayed with me after I landed in Africa, not in a tank with its imagined protection, but literally on my feet with a rifle. These words put a clamp on my mind, enabling me to stand and fight and not just cower in fear. For the more I feared I was about to be killed, the more I would rise up—on my knees, that is, till I got another, and another, and another, not knowing my peak would be in Kasserine Pass, which was very fortunate, because I would never have lasted exposing myself like that, letting hate and determination overcome common sense. Oh, of course, like any teenager, the words of my father didn't really sink in until I could literally look down the throat of the monster coming at me. Not just with my eyes, but encompassing my peripheral vision and ears, my mind! Screaming with each pull of the trigger into the side of my weapon. Get'em! Get'em! Get'em! Get before gotten!

My dad was proud of me; my mother and sisters were crying as I made ready to leave to return to camp. This is when my father took me aside and told me those words that guided me through all the despair and fear I was bound in time to face. Remember, when a Scotchman goes off to war he must have one thing in mind: to get one of the "Buggers" before they get you! If you do, then you'll not have been wasted. Oh yeah! I said, "Sure, Pop, I'll do my best." I'm sorry to say I didn't give much thought to those words until we were really in it and the hairy beast was bearing down. Hey, Pop, look, I got my man. I was home free! From then on his words stuck with me, and the purpose in my mind was to make my death as expensive as possible to the enemy!

Oh, man! I've drifted off again. I'm really not on a soap box telling you how brave I was. What I'm telling is what I promised, the way my mind was working, and not meant to be bragging. Believe me, this next one really became the first and worst hairy beast I ever got tangled with, or ever thought I'd never get away from. None of us thought we would; it would be in "Kasserine Pass." Oh yeah!

Well to get back, if you can still follow me. We were off to Jersey City, our port of embarkation. As we got off the train there were people handing out Baby Ruth candy bars. Each guy got one as we headed for a ferry boat tied to the pier. On the candy wrapper in large letters they had printed, "Good Luck." Oh yeah! Anyway, it was a nice gesture. We were all loaded aboard the ferry until we were standing in every available space. A tug got a line on us, and off we went into New York Bay to board a ship. On the way I heard a real Laurel and Hardy pair: "Laurel" said, "I hope we don't have to stand like this to England," and "Hardy" said, "Don't be so dumb; they probably have beds for us downstairs." That's just a little laugh I put in there, but it happened! I'm still not making anything up. I heard that exchange.

The tugboat took hold of us and took us to the end of a pier in Staten Island. On the trip we got to see dozens of ships in the bay, no doubt getting ready to form a convoy. As we got off the ferry, officers waiting for us chalked numbers on our helmets as we told them our names and serial numbers. Then a short walk, dragging our "barrack bags" to a very big ship; it was really only an average ten-thousand-ton freighter, but of course it looked huge to all of us.

By climbing up a very steep gangway we got on the ship, and according to the numbers on our helmets we were sent to different holds and different decks in those holds. Now, here was my first bit of luck: I wasn't assigned to hold number one, as many of us first off of the ferry were. Maybe they were all of a group, I don't know. I went into hold number two, bunk on the "tween" deck, aptly named as it's between the bottom of the ship and the top. Great! Not a far climb to the main deck.

Holds on ships are where they normally carry cargo. The holds on this ship had been converted to carry men on bunks tiered as high as four to a post. All appeared cosy, but that was to be seen. Then, with all arranged, on December 12, 1942, we set out to cross the Atlantic, the year the U-boats, according to the history books, had their highest scores of ships sunk! Fortunately we didn't know that! (I kept no personal notes. I get my dates off my honorable discharge.) Wasn't that a ball . . . I don't think any of us had ever been out to sea.

Our first day out was fantastic. No world at all, everything was gone! Nothing but ships and water. I was just as "gosh and golly" as any farmer boy. Frothy water sprinkled in your face, the air unbelievably sharp and clean, watching all the other ships sailing their way along the same as we were. We all felt our first time at sea was awesome, with the slight feeling of rising and falling.

Being in an army that's unfortunately forever assailed by orders, and orders, could have its intermittent pleasures, but the first day was only a taste of what it could be. The next morning it was different. The ship wasn't sailing anymore—with high wind and waves it was dancing. It wasn't so much the dips and twists that got you but the shuddering short jerks changing momentarily any direction you might be trying to walk in, imposing the same on the ship. You could wind up on your knees, and of course for those so afflicted, a sickness of unending heaves, accompanied by the feeling of their impending demise. Unfortunately death wasn't just a feeling of the seasick men. It had come aboard in number one hold, the hold that for whatever reason I hadn't been put in. One of the merchant mariners, a deckhand, later told me that on any ship, hold number one will be subjected to the severest gyrations, rising and falling madly because of its being the farthest away from the dampening effect the weight of the engine room has on a severe storm. Assailed from the heaving and tossing of the ship in the mad water, the storm had unleashed hell below. In number one all of the makeshift bunks collapsed, crushing two men to death and breaking many bones of others in the mass of pipes and chains. We were told one of the men had just been married. The rest of our trip was a little more somber. It was the beginning of a fact I was to become aware of as I progressed. Some men went quick, on the sea or the land, lasting only as long as it took to jump off the truck to get the "chop," while others, with incredible luck, were always doing the right thing at the right time, to become, in a way, veritable immortals for a short period.

Something else interesting—losing two men to the storm might have saved all of us because, believe me, if we had ever been called to abandon ship, our positions precluded our immediate escape and would have led to positive drowning. No lifeboats for us, just jump off the ship. Try to swim away from the ship before it sucks you under or a "Carley" float lands on your head. As noted, German charts show that 1942 was the highest scoring year for their submarines. That storm, you might say, could have been like our escort, keeping the heads of those "beloved Buggers" in their beloved submarines, down, way down.

Anyway, I had no fear of storms. Since I never got motion sickness, I never got seasick. And of course it helped that I didn't have brains enough to know any better. (I was still only nineteen.) I enjoyed standing on the "poop" deck (that's the back end of the ship), and when the ship would go from the top of the wave down to the trough, the water would rear way over my head, and then just before it would collapse on me, the ship would rise up and clear me. Whoopee! And we'd do it again. Great scary fun. Hang on, baby. But then, Lordy, Lordy! Later, talking to the merchant marine, he told me that if just one time the water would beat the ship, and I was told it does happen, (it's called getting the ship "pooped") tons of water would have collapsed on deck and I would have been gone! Maybe I should have titled my story "David and Death," because there's much more to come.

Another little thing to tighten the scalp was being down below in one of the holds when our destroyer escorts would drop some "ashcans." We were told most of the times the destroyers were doing this to scare away the submarines. But as you must learn about me, always with the rejoinder, I had to pipe up. Or maybe it's like knocking on the sub's door to tell them where we are.

We were all issued little brown pamphlets on Africa—how we should behave to the natives and not shoot Frenchmen unless they're trying to kill you. That last line is no joke. The French killed quite a lot of our guys before they pulled the old "armistice" bit on us. Then the next drill was abandon-ship practice. "Listen up, you guys. You are assigned to go up on the main deck, midship, starboard side. Be sure to cross your arms over the life jacket, up under your chin so when you jump you don't break your neck when you hit the water."

"What?! What did he say?" And he's not laughing. "What!"

We're all standing goggled-eyed looking at each other. Christ! Did you ever feel your parents didn't love you? Wasn't the U.S. Army and Navy supposed to take care of us? Look how far down that water is. A chorus of voices hollering, "What?! Jump from here? I can't swim!"

"Oh, don't worry, life rafts will be dropped in the water with ya."

Boy, what a kiss off! If your own side will do that to you, what will the Germans do? Are you sure the Germans didn't send this ship over for us? But at least we got life jackets we can hold over our heads so they will protect us when the life rafts land on them! Oh! Just making jokes again. But every word is true! Those were really our abandon-ship instructions.

Converted freighters didn't have life boats for all. Should I say, only for officers? Nah! I didn't find out about that. Anyway, officers deserve better. Oh yeah!

Being down below at my bunk when destroyers would drop "ashcans' to make the ship shudder would make me pay attention to what some guys were saying, how lucky we were to be on a big steel ship. I wouldn't say anything to these guys. Sure, they were farmers and country boys, but remember, in those days we had no television, only radio that played mainly singers and comedians, little news. Well, anyway, we didn't get torpedoed, but we did get into that fierce storm. Oh yeah! Because of the storm, which lasted several days, we got no Christmas dinner; everyone, including the cooks, was sick. All we got was potatoes and bread. I was one of the lucky ones; I never got motion sickness, so I got to eat whatever I could find.

Now something new—this time there was a great hubbub up on deck. We could see the lights of Spain as we were entering the Mediterranean. Terrific! Safe at last. Then, unbelievably, all the ships turned on their deck lights. It was like they suddenly decided to light up the bull's eye, and that was us! Mother! What's happening? And now whistles were blowing, making more noise than New Year's Eve! Whoo-whoo. Great God, we were threatened with death if we so much as lit a match on deck in the dark. Now this! Now, if they're having a party, for what reason could this be? That's it, son of a bitch, the war's over. The Germans found out we were coming over and quit, leaving all us "heroes to be" frustrated. And that's why all the ships are celebrating. What rotten luck! Well, never did find out why they did it (that is, blowing the whistles), but by damn they did do it. Of course, as you know, it wasn't quite armistice. It was more like the passing of another convoy going the other way, and the effort to avoid collisions, with all the necessary whistles and lights. You know, I was going to write "just" another convoy, but one convoy passing through another can't be described as "just." Just ask anyone standing in his stained brown underwear in one of those pilot houses. Oh yes!, Oh yes!

In time we proceeded to dock at "Oran," and as we got off we were handed live ammunition for our rifles. Again, as I explained I was in "Armored" and used smaller hand weapons. The guy with the ammo gave me a look and said, "Oh, sure, I understand. Just see that officer over there, but do me a favor and take the ammo with you anyway."

The officer, in turn, was very nice and agreed there had been a mistake. But right now, infantry was needed and I was assigned to Company A, Twenty-sixth Infantry Regiment, First Infantry Division. And as soon as I got with them, some officer there, he was sure, would see that I was sent to the Armored. "Meantime, Private, if you don't mind, just get up on that truck over there."

Gee, wasn't he nice, addressing me by rank? A perfectly professional kiss off. Lying to the peasants must be a special course officers take at army school. But for me now came the great dawning. It was that beloved sergeant back in Fort Knox. He's the guy! He super scuppered me. Guess he didn't like how our fight turned out. But I ain't fighting no war with a lousy rifle. Jeez, imagine all that sweat and knuckle busting work in ten weeks of training in Fort Knox thrown away. As I stand, I'm sure I'm worth a lot more to my country as a tank man than a common foot-slogging infantry man. Besides, a guy doing that could get killed before he threw so much as a rock at the enemy. But in truth, the beloved sergeant saved my life because at the time the Germans had a weapon called an "eighty-eight" that shot our tanks, including our newest Shermans, to pieces, killing most of the crews, and because of the dearth of trained crews, I know absolutely if it wasn't for the sergeant I was bound to have been in one of those tanks.

Of course, at the time I knew nothing about that. And in my appealing to the infantry company commander to get me transferred back to the armored division, I was told the old army answer, "Don't worry, soldier, it will be worked out." Now, this meant all my tank training was out the window and I had to start learning how to fight on my feet! Little did I know I'd be digging foxholes all across Africa and Sicily! And the M1 rifle was a wonderful piece of equipment, but I had never seen one before. (There are no rifles carried in a tank.) I am not exaggerating. I never saw any rifles in Fort Knox. Even on guard duty you were given a large forty-five revolver, nicknamed "horse pistol," that was carried in a huge holster.

Now to get back. I'm sure I'm not writing well, because I'm always going off into left field, but stay with me. It gets better. Again, lady luck stepped in (that is, for me) in the form of a kid from Manhattan. He was, I believe, twenty-one, and I was nineteen. We were both of the group just dumped off of the ship, and of course both products of the lean years of the Depression. Observing as my uncles had taught me by looking at the eyes of my newfound friend, Solan, there was no bluff there. No long hair or tattoos, raggedy cloths, nothing like the tough-acting boys today with their long hair. With that in my hand, I'd have 'em on the ground with my knees in their chest in a minute. They frown and act as if fat and ugly constitutes "tough." My guys had no need for guns, knives or chains, just fists and feet would do back then. But best of all, my new friend Solan had been through basic infantry training and knew all about the M1 rifle.

With him coming from Manhattan and me from Brooklyn, we were practically neighbors. He was showing me about stripping and servicing the rifle and showing me how to take the World War I packets of thirty-caliber rounds out of their encrusted condition in twenty-year-old cardboard packets so that none of the cardboard clung to the brass of the round (bullet), for if the slightest bit of it was left on the brass it would jam in the barrel of the rifle. Then after one shot you'd be out of business. So it could mean your life to be meticulous and clean each round as best you can before placing it in a clip. (A "clip" is the metal sleeve that holds eight rounds placed in the rifle and is ejected with the firing of the eighth round, telling you that your empty. Which also can tell any enemy the same. So, you better have another clip in your hand ready to go!)

Now I had to learn how to strip and care for the "piece," how to operate the safety. Unfortunately, the only firing practice I got was dry runs. Nothing to shoot at. So far we had been moving a lot and the army had been like a very large Boy Scout camp, with weapons but no shooting, but in time eventually I loaded live rounds Oh yeah! And like my life in the army was always a little "different," unbelievably the first chance I got to *really* fire the M1 was to try to kill a man, and do it! That, I can remember and remember well! I can't remember everything, but I can remember that! How many times had I thought, *How am I ever going to shoot anyone?* I found out in time that this was a decision no guy "in it" needs to make. The enemy will cause it to happen. Easily! Especially when he tries to kill you!

My first memory ashore was an A-rab. He sold me a "fig" bar, and thinking it was like a date bar I ate it down; and boy it really moved me. Wasn't much left in me after that. Gave my beloved bowels exercise for some days; felt like they would be coming out of me! (Bowels, and maybe even teeth, that is.) If ever I saw him again! But they all looked alike to me, running around in dirty sheets and bandaged heads.

Now we were told to pick a partner. Solan and I were naturals, so we became "Solan and Dave." Always to pull details patrols, guard duty and chow together, and never for any reason, short of death, could one desert the other, but of course the implications were lost on two young men.

We were put on trucks and drove all along the coast of Africa to Algeria, then inland to a place called Tebessa. The next thing my pencil can uncover, I was climbing up a mountain trail. We were told to relieve a French garrison. On the way up we passed three French soldiers who had old rifles about eight feet long. When we finally got to wherever we were going, where was the French garrison? Oh, that was those three guys we passed. Funny? Sure, but that was the last laugh we were to get for some time. What happened after that I can't remember. Mostly riding here and there, beating the bushes. We got to believe everything fled before us. The mighty U.S Army.

II INITIATION, "REAL" INITIATION

I call it initiation because from here on the games and fun would end. Abruptly.

Again we unloaded from trucks to go again up a hill, rifles locked and loaded. This time to stop or get reported Italian infiltrators. Here we go again, chasing butterflies with rifles. As we got near the top, we moved over like whitish rock. Back below, where we had left the trucks, whistles were blowing. That meant planes, and we were always to get away from vehicles and take cover when we heard whistles. But we were in no position to do that now. We could only fall flat on the whitish rock and look up at them, watching as the German planes flew over low enough to see the black crosses. Seeing the real stuff, black crosses, enemy directly overhead, sort of put a tremor in your scrotum. Oh mother! We were meat on the table, or more like brown roaches crossing a white table. They didn't fire! They disappeared over the brow of the hill. Oh, man! What luck! Them dumb Buggers didn't see us. Ah! But here comes lesson number one: Germans are not dumb. They have a purpose.

In the time it took them to swing around they were back. Guns blazing, right over our heads; we froze. They were shooting up the trucks we had just come in, then they were gone. Well, man, if you had desired shooting, that sure was it. But I didn't want it while my brown-uniformed ass was out in the open on white rock!

The howling planes and blasting guns, seeing what those guns did to the trucks, left us all frozen and gave us a tremendous boost! We couldn't get to the brow of the hill and out of sight fast enough. Then, before anyone could enjoy being out of sight, guys were yelling, "Tanks! Tanks!" I dropped flat. I ain't running back out there!

And just as I thought, *How could tanks get up here?*, guys who had been up ahead were stampeding over me, over my back and legs, running and falling back down the hill. Of course it proved to be a silly panic (no tanks), but you have to remember we were all still "virgins." And given to panic. Especially after the just passed Luftwaffe demonstration.

The line of guys I was in hadn't run because we were just at the brow of the hill and saw nothing. We were told to keep moving. The guy on my right had been matched up to me as my "buddy." The buddy system was necessary, as we each had a blanket and would put one on the ground and the other over us. But we also shared the thing I grew to hate worse than the Buggers making me eat dirt—guard duty. Endless night sweat. Sharing this with my buddy. I was proud of my buddy because we had just passed a test together. When the guys ahead of us were scared off by "tanks" we held our ground.

Looking back at some of the dumb, green things we did, I mean, our "green" officers and non-coms, it was a miracle we weren't all killed right off! Oh yeah! For the skirmish lines like we were doing we should have had scouts, at least two guys up ahead.

We pushed ahead through like brush and grass crossing over the brow to the other side of the hill. At least we had sense enough to keep spread out. As I passed a thicker clump and some small trees I heard an odd voice behind me. Only then I realized I was still "locked and loaded." Pushing off my safety, I found myself looking at two Italian soldiers. It was almost comical how big their smiles were, there arms stretching up as high as they could go, and they were calling, "By Zon, By Zon." I learned later it meant friend. But my smile turned to shock as I saw that the niche they were standing in front of held a machine gun, tray inserted, ready to go. They didn't use a belt feed, as we did to feed ammo to the guns. They used trays, and they had boxes and boxes of trays, and also boxes and boxes of red devil grenades. I made a wild look behind the gun but there was only the two Italians, who actually had feathers in their helmets. I whistled to Solan, "Look, I got two prisoners!"

Just as he turned, another guy, an Italian officer, popped out of the brush right alongside of him. Standing in the grass, pistol in hand, he shot Solan full in the face. His helmet flew off and he was flung backward, arms spread dead. It couldn't happen; we were only boy scouts playing soldiers. But it did happen, and it happened before I could even move.

Solan and I had gone through the pricking of the finger bit to become "blood brothers," just as we had both seen in the movies. We both knew this time it was for real. We both knew from what little we had seen so far. No more games now, we were soon to face doing what we really did not know how to do. But we were determined to do it! Whatever was to come, it could be faced better with a man pledged to stand with you, and never for any reason would one crap out and leave the other. Now this, our first action and he's blown away before me.

This would never have happened had I not been the green young man I was. Had it been the David of today, no skirmish line would advance without scouts on either flank to avoid surprises, and if the scouts had been Solan and myself, we would never advance standing up. We would have advanced at a crouch, eyes sweeping left and right, also dead ahead for mines. And I would have seen the Italians before they had to call to me. I would have dropped to my knee, while giving a high whistle that my partner would know meant trouble. I would have waved to the two Italians with my rifle to go in front of me, then motioned them to get down. Who knows, they might have buddies wanting to kill them, or me. Now, after all that movement, stay still. Wait, watch, there is a good chance there'll be more of them. Then motion the Italians to move ahead. This way both Solan and myself would have seen the officer rise up with his weapon, and it would have been him who would be caught between two "MIs" before he could fire.

I'm sure the third Italian was a brave man. He didn't put up his hands like the others. He had waited, then shot the man nearest him. Then a point I surely remember—his head twisting over his shoulder, pistol still on Solan, when he saw me. He looked me full in the face, eyes alight, twisted in fear. Or was it hate? As I see it, I know now my anointment was here. From here on out, I was to be bathed in fire fights and death! I was stunned, but by no means numb. *David, David.* My mind went to work. The piece started jumping in my hands. I was pulling and pulling the trigger.

I don't know what he did with the pistol. He fled, jinking as he ran downhill. *No! No! Christ, he mustn't get away! David! Get'em, get'em; don't let him get away.* My mind screamed, aim to the left! *David, don't try to follow his jerks.* Bringing the piece to my eye, rifle sight on his form to the left, sure enough, on his next jink left, I nailed him! His legs flew in the air. He went down out of my sight for a moment. Then as I came up to him, point blank, I pulled the trigger and pulled the trigger until the *ching* of my empty clip stopped me. I didn't want to *just* shoot him, I wanted to tear him apart.

My mind seething, I dropped to my knees as I tried to get a little out of sight to reload. As I did, I turned, looking behind me. I fell back, stunned, as if I had seen the "Heavenly Host" descending. I know I couldn't have been more awestruck. Other guys were helping Solan sit up! Impossible! How could that bastard have missed? Solan's face wasn't even bloody! You can believe I was elated, ecstatic. He was up on his feet. I remembering slinging my rifle and hugging him. My worst nightmare relegated to dream status. How else could I explain a "miracle?" Now we could go on together, and I would never again give anyone a chance to tag his butt.

He told me later that just as heard me yell he turned with his face right in the guy's pistol, saw the flash, felt the blow to his head and chin, and fell backwards. He too was sure he was dead. He was so shocked he felt nothing more until he felt the men lifting him up. It felt like they were lifting him out of a hole. The other guys behind me were slightly uphill, and with my firing downhill they didn't know why or what I was firing at. Until they saw Solan down. They came to his aid and mine. They saw the mess I was kneeling over and just asked what happened. Pushing them aside, I got over to Solan. There I saw the bullet had just fanned his cheek and hit the ring on the inside of the helmet, the ring that holds the chin strap. Then the bullet ripped the outer edge of the helmet like it had been done with a can opener.

Solan was still wide-eyed and working his jaw. That's all I got to see or hear when again the whistles—planes! Where to go? Everything's the same here. Get down, face and fingers in the dirt, no chance to run or get cover. Again the firing! But this time they're shooting up a hill to our front, the hill we never got to, the hill still being held by the Italians. Hey, hey, hey. Everybody on their feet yelling, "Give it to them!" Then the word, "Pass it on, everyone back to the trucks. Pass it on."

We were all turned back from the diving planes. We didn't retrieve Solan's helmet, and I didn't get back to the Italian to look for the pistol. We got back to the top on the hill we had climbed. We saw two of the six-by-sixes burning and a Jeep that was a smoking wreck. To protect us from a fourth visit from them black crosses we went down in sections and as quick as possible. On my way down, who for Christ's sake would believe they flew directly over us three times! Now look! More GI death. On one of the charred truck cabs it looked like the burned body of a boy stuck to the wire ring of what was left of the steering wheel. Like a black mummy. We wondered why the guy hadn't jumped. Guess he had probably caught a bullet right off.

I feel I must reiterate the story of the planes. The planes were not up in the air. If a telephone pole is about thirty feet, then I would say that would make them sixty to seventy feet over us. Not to the side, over us! I have pledged no tall stories, no fillings. They may be hard to believe but I kid you not. No embellishments. (I know that word but had to look up the spelling.) I promise to give you the dope from only one end of the horse! Sure, I'm trying to put in a few laughs as I write. It helps that I remember guys back then saying in some of the worst situations, "Someday we'll look back at this and laugh!" But please pardon me if I don't do it now.

As the euphoria of getting Solan back wore off, I began to think of how close he came to being killed, for nothing. Did anyone know what we were doing? There seemed to be no cohesion; our officers and non-coms seemed to be playing everything by ear. Thinking back now, I guess it was all they could do. No one had any experience. Any experience of combat passed on by an older veteran could only have been experience from WWI, and that was nothing like this—moving men all over the map by truck, ready to attack people of unknown amounts or quality, with one lousy company without so much as another company in reserve. Never mind artillery mortar and heavy machine gun units or any protection from planes (and of course no armor or bulletproof vests). Whoops. Not even the one's that are not thick enough. A GI shirt had to do.

A division. The First Infantry Division is designed to fight as a unit, according to Solan. Three battalions. That's battalions, not companies! Two battalions are committed to fight while the third remains in reserve to come to the assistance of any battalion needing it and to replace any battalions pulling back for rest with artillery and many other forms of fighting, not to mention air-ground support. This is a tremendous fighting force, but . . .

The inexperience went right to the top. Eisenhower himself had no experience. He was a "desk" general, not a fighting one like Patton. Eisenhower was put in charge of the Allied Forces in North Africa, and this left him committed to taking advice from the British "Allied," not American. Already politically correct.

The British had lost every combat they had been in since 1939, thrown out, "evacuated" from every country they went into. And these were the people our top men like Eisenhower were to take advice from. A quote from the British:

"Now then, a two hundred mile front to cover. No problem, chum! Just scatter a single division along it and let them fight by companies."

Imagine Eisenhower's words to his officers! "You're not to think of yourselves as Americans, but as Allies."

Reading this later I understand Patton blew his stack.

And that's what we had been doing, climbing hills, running around chasing phantoms like the "French garrison." We had been getting away with this because the French and Italians were a joke. The same as the Americans were. But the German 21st Panzer Division was about to change that. We were a high school team about to take on the "pros."

Quote: "The North African Campaign was not always successful as in the first few days of counter-attack by German General Rommel at Kasserine Pass in Tunisia the Allies were caught unprepared."

Meaning, I suppose, "brains."

That's the way they put it, in those words. In truth there were two First Division Companies in the pass. My Company "A" and one other. Needless to say, that was no contest. But that's a story to come later.

After Kasserine Pass, Rommel was quoted as saying the American soldier can do much better with better leadership. He picked it out! Leadership! Needless to say, Rommel wasn't taking advice from the British! Now, "Faid Pass" was to be our comeuppance. End of the joke, we were. And now for the bitter, costly lessons of genuine bloody labor pains, to be reborn into a real, fighting team. But now, before the memory of that, you might say, with a little comedy relief, that is as now, but not then.

We were resting. My adrenaline was down, which in turn brought the pain in my wisdom tooth up. A medic had given me some aspirin to crush and rub on the tooth; surprisingly this worked, but only for a time. My lieutenant excused me from guard duty and gave me a pass to go back to our "field train" to visit the dentist. Besides my own weapon, my M1, he had me take a B.A.R.(Browning automatic rifle) back to ordnance to repair or replace as it could fire any time it had a round in the chamber. So when I got on the truck to go back, the black guy driving gave me a look, saying, "What have we here?" Something about my going the wrong way.

With all the artillery, I did have the B.A.R., my rifle and bandoleer of ammo, and a knife in my belt. The knife really wasn't a knife, it was a dagger from WWI that we had been issued. It was a pointed, four-sided blade, all very sharp. The hand grip was solid brass, about four inches long, and a half by one inch thick. The handle also had brass knuckles affixed, with each finger loop having a raised tit. Now that was a mean machine! I remember at home as boys a guy would put a roll of pennies in his fist to give it a harder punch. This dagger surely could break a man's jaw. In fact, break it in pieces.

Note: Just a thought about the black driver. I know I'm supposed to say "African American," but in those days a colored person preferred to be called black because black was beautiful and they were proud of it. We didn't have then what has grown to rule our country, the media. They have reporters everywhere that put the KGB spies or Hitler's Gestapo to shame. Each and every reporter has one goal in mind—to get the "big" story. How about Dan Rather, a *non-elected* reporter of our society, trying to unseat our president. But his contacts failed him; he blew it. They have changed our language to nice words. A jungle is a "rain forest." Imagine, "Tarzan of the Rain Forest." Whoops! How about taking a walk in a swamp! Lovely, if you call it a "wetland." How about all those bums, tramps, vagrants you could take in; they're "homeless!" And now the best, the religious maniacs of Iraq; they're "insurgents." Everyone must have a title. But best of best, they don't just report news, they explain it to us in their, as they call it, "righteous slant." Do you accept all this without question? Congratulations! You've been brainwashed.

Sorry I went off again! Well, anyway, the driver was an okay guy. He wanted to look at the dagger and he remarked it was the meanest thing he had ever seen. I told him the story of how I got one. At first, when we were issued these incredibly ugly, dormant but always ready WWI weapons, we had all laughed because, who would ever use such a thing? But you learn. Wartime is different, and in time you can believe everything gets used. And now, because my tooth was killing me, I had to go back and see the dentist, so please, brother, step on the gas.

He asked what else I had to fight with and I said I kept grenades but I didn't bring any with me. Why did I call the big rifle a bar? I said that's a b.a.r. (Browning automatic rifle), fires twenty rounds in a clip. Our regular rifle, the M1, fired eight rounds from a clip. The Browning could fire one round or all twenty in a burst. But this one was unloaded and I was taking it back to ordinance for repairs.

I thought the driver was completely without care and easy going. But he told me he was afraid that someday when he came up with a load of shells, if the truck got hit they would never find even a piece of him. I told him to look on the bright side of it, that if he was hit he would never suffer. He would never know it. In the mean time he had a truck and could always stash some extra goodies under the seat and never be hungry. I said, "If I know you guys, you already 'won' stuff that's 'fallen' off some other trucks. Under the seat, right now." He laughed.

III

We got back to like a small village where all kinds of supplies and equipment were piled up, and I found ordinance in something like a stone house that had a slate roof. And I have cause to remember the slate roof!

I was explaining to a "tech" sergeant what was wrong with the B.A.R. and a far-superior middle-aged captain broke in saying that what I told them was impossible, and started to give me a lecture on the principals of firearms. But I begged off, explaining my pain and my need to see the dentist. I didn't care about the B.A.R. I had to get to the dentist, then I would be back.

Here I would like to pause and explain to anyone reading this, I'm not trying to put down captains or make my part brilliant. Although it does work out like that sometimes. I hadn't taken ten steps out of the building when BAM! BAM!, two shots rang out and pieces of the slate roof flew in the air. Hot damn! I never went back in, but I hoped he hadn't killed himself. It would have spoiled a good joke. Truly! It would have made a mess. But we had plenty of smart-ass captains.

And now I have to relate my experience with the dentist. Now again, I swear no hyperbole. This is what happened: The dentist had his equipment and operations in an ambulance. The ambulance had taken a near miss; one of the rear wheels had been removed, I guess, to be replaced. The truck itself had holes in one side from whatever had caught it. Some guys with red crosses on their helmets told me the dentist wasn't badly hurt but had gone to a nearby evac. hospital to get some dressing changed and should be back by the afternoon. Afternoon! I could feel the tooth getting bigger! It occupied my whole head!

Now, as my hope had been shattered or at least put off, I guess it showed. Then a tall, skinny guy stepped up and said he wasn't authorized to do it but it seemed to be an emergency; he would try to help me. Now, I wouldn't let just anyone do this, but he was the dentist's assistant and had a gold bar on his shoulder. I found out later a gold bar with a brown stripe in the middle was a warrant officer.

I could see by this skinny officer's eyes that he really wanted to help. Eyes can tell you a lot about a person. His were really sincere. "Okay!" I said, "I'm willing to try anything." And that included probably pulling it.

He said he wasn't authorized to give pain-killing shots. It would hurt, sure, but then I could pack aspirin in the hole and it would be over. He demonstrated how, by using his fist against my jaw as a fulcrum, he could flip the tooth out easy. And that way it wouldn't hurt too much.

Now, with him, an officer, appealing to me, and as I said, I could see he wanted to do this, and the "medic" guys standing around looking at me, I couldn't crap out and say I was afraid! I sat on a gas can with a guy on either side to brace me. The guy dipped the tool in something, got into position, his fist against my jaw, and I was ready for the pull.

In truth, I felt I had been smashed to the ground. Because that's where I was! He had proved his inexperience by not pulling but crushing my tooth! The searing pain had me fighting the guys still holding me. There was a lot of yelling. Guys were holding me as he started sticking needles in my mouth and holding something over my face. Whatever it was he wasn't authorized to do, he was doing it now. Gradually I felt my jaw getting numb, then my ears getting warm, then my head was floating. Then I felt I was standing over myself, watching, amused and laughing as he was picking pieces out of my mouth. I can't say how I got back to my outfit, and as I promised I won't fill in with made-up stories, but I do remember going back laughing all the way.

My officer wanted to know why I didn't bring the B.A.R. back, and how did I get blood all over myself? Solan told me later that he had asked me things, but I don't remember. But I do remember when all the dope or whatever he stuck into me wore off my jaw; it felt like it had been punched hard and I had to eat "Sippy" for awhile.

As I read over this, it's like I've written a funny story. Well, I guess after sixty years you could call it that! That's good if you can laugh, enjoy! They become infrequent.

IV COMEUPPANCE AT "FAID PASS"

After our reserve rest we loaded on the trucks again. This time it was going to be no more second-rate teams; the Germans were waiting for us at "Faid Pass."

Our generals were still doing it, taking advice from the losers. But this game the British couldn't lose. If the advice they gave was bad and resulted in failure, well, chum, it's because the American soldier is green or can't fight! Now, if the advice is good and the fighting goes well this time, chum, it's because of great British intelligence and advice. A joke? No, thank you. It cost too many American lives.

Again, we went by truck to someplace no one had ever heard of, "Faid Pass." This from the beginning was a little different. When the trucks dropped us off we had to march about half a mile up a macadam road. This is a bit difficult to write slowly because David knows what's coming.

David was annoyed because he had to pull a cart. As we had de-trucked, as they called it, the lieutenant hollered, "Solan, you and Dave get on this wagon."

What he meant was the small ammunition cart. We were to take a hold of the oversized t-shaped handle and pull it along on the macadam. It was easy, but it took both of us to pull over dirt. We had shouldered our rifles and tagged along. Another officer was directing who should go where and advising everyone not to go farther up the macadam, which was under enemy observation. Enemy observation? We had been told this time we were to displace an enemy patrol. And they had observers?

Now, I can't tell what followed in exact sequence, but all of the action is exactly what to the best of my ability actually happened.

We went through some trees as we were directed to the left, which I would say was east. This time there was no hill to climb, some brush and bushes, but mainly flat. And to the south, the reported position of the enemy, we could see at the most a mile away. The ground rose, and this time we got a great surprise. There were about six half tracks with mounted 75mm pieces. These, we thought, were the greatest; any enemy tank in their sights would be blown away. I was the only one in the outfit who had been trained at Fort Knox and I could tell the guys how the pictures of German two- and three-man tanks with 37mm or 57mm weapons had been shown to us, and these half tracks would be hitting them before they even got in range of our half tracks and tanks. And the new Sherman would eat them alive. And you've got to believe, I couldn't wait to see this happen. I'm hot to trot.

Unfortunately in 1939 those little two-man German tanks had conquered France, which at the time had the largest standing army in the world sitting behind impregnable fortresses (I think it was called the "imagine that" line! What crap!) and a larger navy than the Germans. And tanks! The French had more tanks and larger tanks. Yet all this power was a fraud. Like "French honor," they crapped out in a week. Even little Belgium fought longer. Again, if you should think I'm lying or exaggerating, look in your history books! I award the French my deepest flatulent salute. To any French soldier who really fought, or killed some of the Buggers, I apologize.

With this move by France, they had handed over to the Germans their women and children, their old folks, their mothers and fathers, everything in life a man could hold dear, including their military might. This unbelievably was given to the Germans without a fight in an "armistice." I don't speak French, but "armistice" can only mean "surrender" and "slavery" and "being paid in French franks printed in Germany."

I'm sorry I went off on that! And one last disgusting fact—after the war, and as of now, the French government charges the American government for tending the graves of American soldiers buried in France. If ever a country owed another a debt of honor, and they repay it with charges for our dead!

Now, with the fall of France, German manufactures could relax and let the French provide basic war materials. The Germans could now concentrate more on tanks and planes. And best of all, an anti-aircraft weapon called an "88" that could be adapted to be used against tanks. Our Grants and the newest Shermans had no chance against it.

Now to go back to where I said "unfortunately." I meant, unfortunately, in the interim between the French surrender and our arrival in 1942, the Germans had developed many more guns, tanks, aircraft and mines—weapons that now put ours to shame. And they were waiting to give us a demonstration at the other end of "Faid Pass."

We came through the band of trees and I would say another two hundred yards out into an open field, about one hundred yards below and in front of the line of 75mm half tracks. There everyone was told to take off their overcoats and put them in a pile by the ammunition cart. Then the lieutenant told Solan and myself that we were to guard the coats and ammunition until he sent someone back to get the cart if they needed it. I spoke up and said we had pulled it there, couldn't he have two other guys guard it? I remember, "No, no, no. Do as you're told! We shouldn't be long anyway." I remember those were his exact words, because in about two hours, everybody would be running for their lives.

Just then, while the company was still in sight, everyone started yelling and jumping, waving at a row of the twin-tailed American fighters. With those lovely white stars. This was a tonic. For once we were to get help from the planes and the half tracks. The planes had been just to the west of us. Now they made a sweeping turn over the telephone poles on the road we had come up on. And headed south, toward the Germans. I didn't see what the planes did, but I was very dismayed at the amount of black flack that flew up around them. But very happy that none of them appeared to be hit.

I turned to Solan and sarcastically said, "That's a German Patrol?"

My company started off to the south and we watched them go with some trepidation. Seemed mighty lonesome, even in broad daylight. I had noticed something odd about the half tracks. I hadn't seen anyone around them. Where could those guys be? You'd think with all this action they would be getting ready. Maybe they're in foxholes. Or buttoned up in their vehicles. Thinking I might bum some better chow from them, I walked up to them. They weren't buttoned up! They were wide open! There were things scattered about. I hollered, "Hey! Anybody home?" Silence. Jeez! How could they all run off and leave this?

I got the sudden, tickling urge to back off and run; something wasn't kosher. What if they had all been captured! Suppose Company "A" had been sent here to protect these guns, and the Germans had gotten there first! Maybe that's why the lieutenant seemed so agitated.

I started to climb on one to see if the guns had been disabled. Solan gave our sharp whistle. Solan and I had practiced a whistle, high, sharp and brief. We never whistled for fun or hello; it always meant something urgent. "Look out!" I jumped down and ran back. He was on the ground pointing. Oh, man! Now what? Look, Dave! Tanks are coming at us from behind! Hey! Hey! A Sherman! I hollered, "Hey, man, that's ours."

As the tank came toward us I saw another behind it. And another behind that. I was bursting with relief. Here we had gone from two men being left alone with a pile of overcoats, some spare ammunition and some unmanned anti-tank guns to two guys surrounded by twenty-four Shermans! And six possibilities of tank destroyers. Not to mention the American fighters overhead! I'm thinking, that's power!

The down side, the big down side, I told Solan, was that I should have been fighting in one of those tanks of ours, not climbing around with a lousy rifle. As they came toward us, the first tank passed us a ways, then stopped and turned to the right (south). The next one came on and did the same, and so on, until I counted twenty-four. We stood just behind the line of tanks. No laughs or waves; these guys were serious. But they were doing something they were not supposed to do. They were spreading out, moving forward like the cavalry. I had learned a word at Fort Knox, "defilade." When tanks move forward, advance, they're suppose to do so by a "hop-scotch" movement. Tanks go from one defilade position to another. That's where the main body of the tank is concealed, with only the turret and main weapon exposed. Then they advance like jumping jacks; the first tank takes up a "defilade" position, covered by the second tank. The second by the third, and so on, so that any enemy gun firing at them would be immediately blasted by covering guns. Now, as they moved forward like the cavalry, I thought they must have changed the rules.

Note: I didn't write about Solan and myself being at the pivot of these turning tanks, to put him and me in the picture. I wrote that because that's the way it happened. And my questioning the formation of the tanks was not to show how smart I am. It's just the way it comes out sometimes. We were taught procedures at Fort Knox, and for whatever reason they were not following them.

And here, if I can judge it, my life was about to change. We had been, you might say, hunting deer or bear, and now we were to turn up something different. Something damn different, like you could say an elephant with big teeth and hoary legs with claws coming at us. We were to unearth "Dragons." A damn nest of them, nothing less. Nothing less! Impervious to any of the toys we had come to fight them with. The pitiful 37mms of our light tanks against 88mms of the German anti-tank guns. The Sherman's thirty tons against the Tiger's sixty tons. Our vaunted weapons could make no more impression on the Germans than a beautiful girl would in a room full of blind men.

Dragons were the mythical monsters that sprang into my mind. It couldn't be anything less, after what I was to see, and no one could convince me that anything less could do. Sure, it was only the well-versed Twenty-first Panzer Division. But we had unknowingly charged into its lair. And many men and much equipment were about to pay for our first lesson.

We didn't have long to wait. Out of nowhere there was a sudden, Ripp, Bam, Boom; another Rip, Bam, Boom.

What the hell's happening? You could feel the rush out of something alongside or over you. Ripp, Bam, Boom. The Germans evidently let our tanks come right up to them. Then, with who knows how many tanks and 88s, they cut loose. The Ripp with the all-but-physical swish you felt was the round passing close by us; the Bam was it exploding behind us; and the Boom was the gun firing in front. And these were only the rounds that missed our tanks! Eighty-eights worked like giant rifles, and at the highest velocity. You know what velocity is? It's when a piece of straw, as shown on TV, driven by cyclonic wind, as in a tornado, can be driven through a plank.

Their shells were 88mm, with the highest velocity and tungsten cores, tungsten the hardest of metals. The 88, firing straight and level across the ground, instead of up in the air like artillery, pierced our tanks and blew them up. Each tank hit sent a spiral column of black, greasy smoke shooting upward, and there were columns and columns. Each one can't be a tank! Oh, good God! It must be something else! Oh yeah!

The only feeling I have ever felt like that since was watching the Twin Towers collapse; my eyes telling me something my brain can't accept. It's got to be something else! It can't be our tanks! What's doing this?

I remember looking at Solan; he gave me a palms-up signal of doubt, shaking his head. We had been standing dumbstruck; we could have been torn apart by one of those misses.

Solan dropped down with a whistle, pointing. Tanks! More tanks coming at us. Oh, Christ!

We're both down, playing dead. What else can we do? Then, through the dust and smoke, it's a Sherman. Terrific! Now we have a chance. Five of them came up, flaying dirt, roaring, passed us as we remained transfixed, fortunately out of their way. Then they turned back to the highway.

The Ripp, Bam, Boom stopped. Now something else. Running men! This could be German infantry following up. What can we do? Can't make a run for the trees, too far; we'd never make it. Looks like payback time. I looked at Solan. We had gotten to the point of talking more by looks and hands than speech. He frowned, nodded, hiking his rifle, dropping on his elbows. What? I shook my head no! You're crazy, no way. I can feel my pencil pulling at my scalp. Christ, look at what's coming! Just my luck, I had to get a crazy partner. Or maybe his near kiss of death flipped him. I was starting to back away, pointing to the mob coming at us.

No, wait! That's it. It's a mob. They're spread out all over. Look at them; one just fell down. It was our guys, all kinds of guys. The guys in tanker coveralls were the worst, burned, bloody, clothing torn, black faces, clothing still smoking. Wild men!

I remember standing unconsciously. I had my piece on a guy, still thinking of getting in my last shot.

This guy howled at me, "What are you doing? Aren't you Americans?"

I waved him down. Easy, pal, Easy! It's true, many insignificant memories pop up, and you have to wonder why. But there, there. Fortunately, many of the real bad ones go the other way, and disappear.

Those five tanks that came back, that was it? I know there were a lot of columns, but nineteen? Nineteen tanks blown away?

I remember pushing my way through all these frightened guys and walking wounded. I'm trying to look for more of our tanks. There must be more. Again I got that awful feeling. I'm holding my piece in my hands so hard my fingers hurt. I was so uptight and vengeful I didn't know to do. Not a German in sight. What's behind all that smoke down there? What did the tanks run into? A fortress? Can't see any more columns of smoke because the whole area is smoke with flashes of flame and exploding ammo. Can't say how my mind was; my world turned upside down. With Solan being shot it was rage. But this, this was stupefying.

Nineteen tanks, five men in a tank, that comes to almost a hundred men lost in the tanks alone, wiped out by that mysterious Ripp, Bam, Boom. There seems to be an awful lot they didn't tell us about at Fort Knox. Here we were, like a man who went to chase a dog and instead ran into a grizzly. If our General Whoever thought it was only an armed German patrol, why the need for twenty-four tanks? And if they thought it was more than that, why no scouts or reconnaissance ahead before getting the whole column wiped out? It was bad enough that the Germans could do this. But by our unbelievably poor leaders, we made it easier for them.

Sure I'm blaming our officers. As a guy just turned twenty, what did I know? I can only thank God that I wasn't where I should have been, in one of those tanks. Instead I was on foot with only a rifle. Still not happy, but happy enough to shake my piece and crow, "I'm still here! I'm still here! Monsters be damned."

But this wasn't the way it was supposed to be. My crowing has turned into a croak! The cowboys have lost!

V

Solan is pulling at my arm; we're being called back, back to the trucks. Our guys are all coming back. I feel ashamed. Now I'm like the others; I'm ready to get away. I click on the safety on my piece, surely a sign I've given up. How can you fight something you can't see? At least we've lost that damn ammo cart! Let a German pull on it for awhile. I guess you think dumb thoughts under stress.

I climb on the truck. All I want to do is sleep. I lay on some gear, exhausted. Last thing I remember is the bouncing of the truck taking me away from this overwhelming mad house. The next day, or whatever day (my mind is a little blurry here), there are tanks, artillery, anti-aircraft guns, truckloads of men, all pulling back the way we had all come. We're told to get everything on the trucks; we're pulling back, back west.

This isn't right. We're supposed to be the greatest. Shit! I haven't even seen a German, and we're retreating! An officer tells us this is not a retreat. The Germans have broken through behind us and we have to go back to help. Oh yeah! I didn't hear about this from just anyone; an officer told me this to my face.

Now another day, again in back of a truck. When it stopped the sergeant called out some names, and two guys dropped off to guard something along the road. And the next stop was ours—"Solan, Dave." Oh yeah!

We had come to what was called a river bed. And the road crossed the river (when it was there) on large flat stones placed in the river bed. This way it couldn't be carried away with a sudden surge of water. And when the flood was over it would still be there. There was an engineering officer there; he explained how he had some men up a ways on the hillside with a machine gun to protect his men working on drilling holes in these large blocks to blow them up. And he needed rifle men to protect the machine gunners from any snipers. Or whatever. That was it; there were no further instructions.

Now, of course we should have dug in on one side or the other, or above it. Not knowing any better, we dug in right in front of it. About fifty feet lower. Of course, in hindsight this was like trying to protect a target by standing in front of it. But our luck held. Later in the day we were picked up and moved along to join the company in chow.

The next day we were told we were in "Serene Pass." (Would it have been ever thus!) But it meant nothing at the time anyway. Just another pass. There would be two companies in the pass itself and two to hold the north shoulder. That was us. We loaded up our packs, ammo belts, bandoleers, and some extra stinking C-rations. When we started up, I can't say. But we did start up. It was the hardest climb so far. And I thought, *The German infantry will have a much harder climb with us firing down at them.* It never occurred to me they might have an easier way up there. In Kasserine. Oh yeah!

When we got to where we were going, it was like a plateau, with a "wadi" running north-south. Here we used the wadi plus foxholes to form a dug-in skirmish formation. Facing east, we were told if the Germans attacked, they would have to come this way, from the east.

Solan and I were at the extreme south end of the line, that is, the right-hand flank. Farther on the plateau ended. And no one could come from that direction. Or so we thought, because no one like a non-com or officer had bothered to look!

I remember it was a nice day. I had put my rifle on a rock or a stump. The bayonet glistened in the sun. It was a new one. Short, not like the WWI long bayonets that unbalanced the piece. We were taking our time digging a foxhole for us both. This way we could man the top of the wadi, and if we came under fire we could drop into the foxhole for protection. I can't remember much of what we did there, except I had two grenades. We had all been issued two grenades. The problem was they were all bright yellow! Certainly nothing you would want to hang on your ammunition belt suspender as tough guys in the movies always did. If you carried them, you had to hide them under your shirt or in a pocket. So what I did, I placed them behind me, like on a dirt shelf of the wadi wall, covering them with some sprinkled dirt so they couldn't be seen. But I knew they were there for whenever I would need them. And of course, like the bayonet, I promptly forgot about them.

The story of the yellow grenades was twofold. First, they were old World War I grenades painted yellow to be used in the States for training. And since that was all they had at the time to send overseas with us, we had, as usual, to make do. And the second story was that they were old World War I grenades painted yellow because they contained "poison gas," and if the Germans caught you with them they would hang you to the nearest tree by the appendage between your legs. Oh well!

As a rule, I'm only able to remember things that gave me cause to remember, but in this instance my memory is right on because it was just at 10 a.m. when we started getting some shell fire. Then— I'm doing my best because everything was mixed up—I heard a sergeant, I think it was, bellowing, "Shoot! Shoot, you dumb bastards. That's them in white!"

He grabbed a man's rifle and started firing it right over the heads of Solan and myself. East, hell! They're hitting us from the south.

Now that put Solan and me not on the flank but at the head of the whole damn company firing south. Fortunately it was over our heads due to the slope we were on. Then we were catching mortar, bullets, whatever! I was trying to reach my rifle and at the same time save a small amount of soup I had put on a small can of gasoline-soaked dirt we used to heat it. And here again a miracle of uncovered memory by my pencil. When Solan and I had gotten away, still running the next morning, we came across a full carton of Camel cigarettes in some guy's abandoned pack. Later on we smoked some to kill the hunger, but thinking back, I never could remember where we got the matches to smoke, because when shrapnel knocked down dirt and rocks, dumping the soup and cans, in my mind everything had been lost, including the matches. But I had put the matches back in my pocket, and after that, when I couldn't move my arm, I had Solan take them out and keep them. And for sixty years I could never remember because of the agony of my right arm. I had written off the matches with the soup, when it had been Solan, not me, who had the matches. (I know this means nothing to the action, but it does demonstrate how when writing out something you know happened, details you have forgotten completely will come out on the end of your pencil. Or mine, anyway.)

I'm sorry, again the pencil jumped the track. But to get back to Solan and our slit trench. I know this small attack started just after I looked at my watch wondering when these guys were going to show with our chow. It was just before 10 a.m. We decided to heat up a can of some kind of muck we had, when the shelling started. I didn't save the soup but I did get to hug my rifle to me to keep the action out of the dirt.

The sergeant yelling about people in white and his firing right over our heads, that meant people coming ninety degrees off where we expected. I was at the bottom of our hole trying to get my shoulders and knees up into my helmet. It was a good thing this was only a spoiling attack or I would have surely gotten a round through the top of my helmet! The people in white, we learned, were Arabs digging holes for the Germans.

I rose up out of the hole spitting dirt and curses, furious with myself. Everything had happened so fast, and trying to save myself I didn't fire even one round. I could have been shot like a cowering chicken! That's right, a cowering chicken! Say it again; make me feel it. Yet here I am! Here I am! Covered with crap, standing on my rifle. It's not possible! I'm standing on my rifle. My piece. I'll have to clean it quick! Maybe I bent the barrel.

There's a lot of yelling, changing our line to face more south than east. I asked Solan if he got anything. He said, no, because of all the firing all around our heads he had to duck too! Well, that makes me feel a little bit better. But maybe that's why he said it.

Now there's worry about the chow and ammo. Those guys might have just walked into it. No one knew at the time there were more Germans behind us than in front! About the only thing I gained by my jackass dive was that I still had a full ammo belt. This is when I heard the lieutenant and the sergeant talking about only a "spoiling attack," and how the next time they would be back in force. And I thought, *Good! I'll be able to make up for what I did, if it kills me!* Oh yeah! Big talk. But if it's true they'll be back in force, at least I'll be ready and not panic.

All I can remember after that was stripping my rifle and Solan digging a different hold for himself. I didn't move because I was in the supposed middle.

I notice my pencil seems to forget things, little things, when it knows that what's coming next is a much hairier beast! Them! They're crazy, coming at us again!

In truth, the hairy beast landed on us just after 2 p.m. In the hell of trying to kill these people through a hail of shrapnel, dirt, stones, mortars and hand grenades (potato mashers), determined to stick it out (I did it!), I had picked a stone sticking up out of the ground like a miniature of the one's at Stone Hedge as likely spot for a man to use as cover as he came over the crest of the rise about a hundred or hundred fifty feet in front of me. All I could think of as I fired was that if he went over backwards I was firing high, and if he stumbled and fell forward I was low. Of course this could be caused by others firing too! Who cares! I was elated! Hell, Dad, I had counted to nine, like at a shooting game at Coney Island, counting as people threw gravel and garbage in my face. Or at least that's what it felt like. I couldn't remember anymore.

Something hit my left foot like a hammer; I had been shot. I was sure my good luck had ended. It won't be long now.

It was slowing down. They had stopped coming, only the occasional crack of a German or the Bam of an American rifle. I was disappointed; I wanted more. I was up on the Dragon's back watching them jump! That gray matter in my skull had gone through a complete metamorphosis. Remember Alice in Wonderland? Once she stepped through, everything was backwards; the armed boy scout, coming through the fire, had shed his skin to become what you wanted. A tough fighting solider. Mercy only to his own. None for any others. Yeah! Now no more ducking! Stand up and fight! You could just as easy be killed taking cover in a hole. Oh yeah! Want to put them Buggering bastards down? Keep your head up, to hell with cover.

I rolled over onto my back to take a look at my foot. There stuck right in the middle of my arch, just above the sole, was the flattened remains of a spent bullet. Being a ricochet it hadn't penetrated the tough cowhide, but the foot was sure sore.

Now there was turmoil. If they hit us again we were in big trouble. More men were sent to get the ammunition we needed. A machine gunner, a young guy, was crying bitter tears; they were taking the rounds out of his belts and passing them around to fill the clips of the riflemen. A sergeant doing this said every round would be aimed fire, not sprayed. The young guy was given a clip and a dead guy's rifle and told to make the piece even the score.

Solan asked me if I had another clip. Then I realized I had only what was left in my piece. Then, looking at me (scout's honor!), he wanted to know what happened to my eyeglasses? I thought something had stuck to my left lens. There was a hole in the lens! The hole was almost dead center of the lens, and it was the size of the hole a BB would make. I remember the *flit, flit, flit* of the shrapnel as it zipped into the ground and my picking up a tiny piece that had hit the ground right in front of my nose. I wanted to see what it looked like, but before I could I had to fling it away; it was red hot. That couldn't have been the one that made the hole because that one hit lower than my chin. The only thing that made sense was one of those bits of steel at high velocity (there's that word again) must have missed the skin of my temple by a hair and drilled a hole through the back of the lens, not shattering it. I know writing about it now it seems like a tall tail. But I don't have to make up any tall tails; I have enough to fill a book. I remember sitting, looking at the glasses, disgusted, wondering, *What the hell next, for Christ's sake?!*

Now, I'm told the word "Christ" should not be used in vain. VAIN! How could anything mean more to me? Appealing to the only power that could appease the "Dragon," only because it's one of the things I remember, I put it down.

Now, after being disgusted with "what's next," it wasn't too bad; I could still see pretty good. And we were soon to forget that. There were many other things to do. I did get another clip, but that was all. There wasn't even any more grenades. I tried to build a little shelter to each side of where I had decided to lay prone if there was another rush. I had fired at the stone, dead center, and it hit at the base, no windage. That meant I would have to fire at a man's head to hit him in the gut. Oh yeah! I took the ugly WWI dagger off my belt and stuck it in the ground next to me. I had been taught to shoot by the owner of a shooting gallery in Coney Island. He said, forget aiming, keep both eyes open, and watch where your shot falls, then compensate.

Now all we could do was hope they wouldn't come again until morning. We had been told Germans didn't like to fight at night. Oh yeah! By morning we should have more ammunition. But NO! It was just getting dark, and at 7 p.m. they came again. More than ever, more yelling! I was ready; I wasn't scared; I was passed being scared. If I remember right, I was more determined than ever. At least that's what I think as I write this.

It's tough writing about being on the wrong end of the stick. Maybe it was more than me. Maybe it was my Scotch genes, determined to get what I can as long as I can, because you can't get out of this. In truth, I can't remember the whole thing. My memory comes in spurts. Firing into the Dragon's face, then as the firing started to slow to a stop, as we ran out of ammo, all of it, I backed away, forgetting I had a bayonet. With the last *ching* of my ammo clip, I backed up to the far side of the wadi. Jesus! What! What now? I threw away the rifle. What good was it? I put up my fists. I was really bewildered. I was getting ready to fistfight; this stupidity no doubt saved my life.

Germans were in the wadi with us, yelling and shoving. One coal skuttle had his piece on me. Now I knew I was going to know how it felt. But it didn't come! There was a lot more yelling, and this guy on me pointed with his piece at my middle and then at the ground. After he did it a second time, I got it. I saw others dropping empty ammo belts, and I did the same. I could see this coal scuttle's eyes were wide and wild. Do it, you beloved bastard, do it! Still wondering, why didn't he shoot? He must have seen his dead and wounded buddies, I mean comrades, out there.

Next there came loud sucking, shells, shells on shells; the place erupted. Shell fire, heavy shell fire. It had to be our side doing it; the Germans wouldn't shell their own men. Thinking, good double damn, why didn't they do this before! Now our ass is history. Next will come my death, for this death is here in person. This death has a face, the face of an infuriated enemy soldier glaring out from under his coal scuttle. He's hesitating; he's cringing from the shell fire. It don't bother me; I'm already dead. He'll shoot me for sure, he has too. Look! He's scrunching up, rifle and hand coming up to his face, eyes wide, mouth wide, his head jerked up. He's thrown himself down. What! Was he hit? Kill him! Kill him! What! With what? No! Not now. Don't try it, get away, get away, there's too many of them. Everyone's down except me. My leg is warm. Now damn, I've pissed my pants. Shelling's terrific. To hell with cover. I'm going to run, even though I may still get shot.

Suddenly the ground begins to really erupt. It's closer, must be almost on top of us! There was the sssucking and whanging of piano chords, blasting stones, big stones, and dirt flying, screaming and yelling, most of the shrapnel fortunately flying over the wadi we were in. If one of those shells found the wadi, it would be good-bye, Mary!

I came alive. It's a gift from the Gods! Allowing us to run, run! Hell, we'll be killed! So what! Shit! Look what we did to those other Germans; they'll kill us anyway! The Germans were all hunkered down. Do it! Go! Go! I may get shot but I'm not going to be anyone's prisoner! Like hell!

I remember as a boy reading the things our beloved Native Americans did to prisoners, crushing, cutting, burning, laughing as they tore out eyes or tongues. Prisoners were left standing on their stumps, the burned stumps of their legs. Howling for mercy. My mind told me then, if ever I'm to be killed, go out killing. Kill. Never be a prisoner! Never surrender your body.

Showered by bits and pieces of dirt, splintered stone hit me in the face. Get down, get down. I was so paralyzed with fear even after I heard the shelling with that loud sucking sound at the start that I couldn't move. My mind's blown a fuse. Concentrate! There's screaming and yelling. Somebody is hit. Biting the dirt, I yell, "Solan! Solan!" He couldn't possibly hear me, but he looks up. I must be able to reach him mentally, or is it just a coincidence? I pump my fist and arm up and down, a sign to move quick.

As I dove down to start to crawl, I saw the hilt of my dagger sticking up out of the ground. I had forgotten about it. I scooped it up, grasping it tight in my fist as I squirmed flat on the ground to get out. To hell with the beloved cover. Madly scrambling to crawl, I'd rather be killed running. Try and stop me, Buggers, I'm going to make it!

I've reached the top of the side of the wadi. Not with any joy—I'm expecting a bullet in the back at any moment if I don't get over the top. Then, oh, Lord, jeez, disaster! Another one! Another Bugger! Rising up almost like a bad dream, another coal scuttle Bugger hugging the top of the wadi as he raised his head to take a look. Instead, he looked right at me, face to face. I exploded, screaming, "Get away, get out of my way!" Raising up on my shoulder, I'm gonna kill one last Bugger, I have too. I feel trapped, having to fight my way out of here. I needed to batter him out of my way. The Buggers behind me couldn't all be distracted!

I had just turned twenty, and I'm sure was in the peak of my strength. Lying flat, swinging my arm with maniacal intent, my fist was guided by the many fistfights through childhood in Brooklyn. Forgetting the brass knuckles on my fist, and with more focused intent than I ever had in my life, I shoved myself forward with the blow, right to the side of his eye. I felt my fist go into his face. Into it, like I had punched a rotten melon. My God! A man's head can't be that soft! What's happened? I scrambled with my left hand to push him away. His helmet had come down on my hand, the hand with the brass knuckles. Throwing the punch I had forgotten all about the dagger, and the dagger with the four fingers of my hand was fully engaged in his skull. That monster lump of brass and steel had smashed his skull! Holy hell! It was caught in his head. Oh, God! The Dragons got me! Super panic. Screaming. I had to get away from here, this hellish place where the Germans had broken through.

I'm calling them Germans this time, not Buggers, because it took real powerful soldiers to do what they did, climbing over broken rock while we fired into them. Hard, brave, or maybe even stupid? But that's all the credit I'll give them, because they were our bitter enemies.

Solan, God bless him, if I remember right, dove on me, wrestled me free. And doing so, we tumbled back down. Christ! Not back down to the feet of the Germans! Solan kept pulling and shoving me, and we scrambled back away down the wadi. We made like monkeys, on knuckles and knees, with dirt, stones and howling shells in the air.

Something was wrong with my right arm. It just hung there. I didn't feel any pain, but it wouldn't hold up.

Now I had surely visited the pit of human emotions. My only thought had been to kill one last Bugger before I got mine; mine couldn't be much longer in coming. The "Dragon" surely was breathing down my neck. What's holding him back? Why the tease of holding my hand? Have your fun, Dragon! I'm still here! I'm still here, you bastard! Sure, I talk to the beast; it's his cage that I'm in, isn't it? Crazy? Sure it helps! And how about another yell I have: Hey, Dad, I got another one! Great! Great! But I'm Dragon meat for sure. But I'm ahead, way ahead.

Now I've really lost count. Now I've reached "GO." I'm home free. No matter when I may be killed, I'm way ahead. I feel like a hornet the DDT has just missed. I'm raving to sting! I've been dropped into this madhouse to fight for my life, and beyond doing it I've enjoyed doing it. And bursting with adrenaline ready to do more.

Unfortunately, in our haste to get away, I lost the dagger. Now we have nothing. Scrambling, it's like we're sliding down the steep side of a house with a roof made of broken slate, rocks and dust. We can just about see. I guess the sun has gone now. When we had gotten some distance away, I felt like my arm had been hit by a bat. The first time I realized I had been hurt, by whatever, or maybe it was that punch, "Solan, I think I've broken my arm." I could hardly move it. That punch meant my life; I put everything I had into it. I'm sure if I had hit a brick wall like that I would have knocked one loose. I know the way I'm writing may seem disconnected, but this is the way it comes to me. Not only that, but going back in mind can bring buried hackles up again. It comes to me not always the way I would like to remember it. I'm amazed at my memory, or is it the pencil? Honestly, As I write my mind is doing two things: trying to spell correctly and thinking of what is coming next. I didn't know I could do that.

Solan and I both knew we had to get away before daylight. If we were found they would not let us go again. Or maybe they hadn't let us go, maybe they had just missed an opportunity. It was real dark now. We had to go north; south was the desert. I remember coming over on the ship, on deck, in the black of night, my face being lit with the millions of stars lighting the sky. The big dipper, or the little one, I'm not sure which, I was told always pointed south. And there it was. Thank you, Lord. Thank you. Unfortunately the only way north meant climbing more mountain, but it had to be done. We found what looked like a path; it was angling up about four or five feet wide, going up the side of the cliff. It was a struggle, trying to grasp, using only one arm. But fear of retribution is what gave me strength.

Then, just as I thought we were getting to the top, listen. Voices! Burbling voices. What? German voices, and a lot of them. How did they get up here so soon? Sounds like a lot of them. We've got to go back down. I'm not tired; I'm just close to hysterical trying to get away from these Buggers before I'm caught again. Now at least I can hold on to Solan with my left arm. I even wish we could go a little faster. But my faith is with Solan. Solan is my buddy; he has saved me before and he can do it again. Now it's his turn to have cat's eyes. He suddenly stops, then, squeezing into a cleft in the wall, pulls me in after him. Germans! I hear them coming. Solan! Holy hell! Pull me in farther. He pulls me more, with all the strength he has in his one arm. But my face is still even with the rock. Trapped, son of a bitch. Trapped for sure. There's no back door to this!

Writing this down I can see myself. I can even feel the ripple across my heart as I write this down. My teeth are clamped, jaw tight. Dad! I may not talk to you again, but if this is it, then add one more Bugger to go with me! What can I say? I try to loosen my body from the clinging rock. The first guy who sees me I'm going to butt off the cliff, and however many more I can, if possible. Brave? Not in my mind. Scared? Now you're talking, but not crawling scared, more like mindless, vicious scared. Determined. Butting an enemy to death with piss in your pants isn't very lofty. You might even say it stinks. Bracing my feet, I feel weird; my body is tingling almost with rapture. My God! The knowledge of what I'm about to do, which can't be avoided, is such a sensation I can feel myself getting hard. Is this to be the ultimate ecstasy?

The jabbering is getting close. I'm up on my toes, trying not to pant. I'm ready. Good-bye, Mother. Then, what! What the hell! What's this? All I can see is the moon shining on the back of a helmet and then the collar of a coat. The guy doing all the jabbering is coming at me backwards! And seems to be lugging something. Soup! Soup! I smell its heady aroma. Truly, no lie, we pass cheek to cheek; he's got his eyes on his buddy, or what they call comrade, guiding him, and his comrade is all eyes on the edge of the path. Oh, God, thank you. Christ, thank you! Is there more? No, I don't see or hear anything else. Thank you, Jesus. Thanks to my Dragon. Good Christ, it's a good thing I'm enclosed by this cliff; my legs have turned to jelly, and I'm gulping air trying not to stutter as I explain to Solan what's happened. I feel sick; I feel empty inside. I'm shaking, still wondering if there's more coming. If there is, I've got to keep quiet and turn my face into the rock to make it harder to be seen. I can still do my pushing if I'm pulled out.

Boy, what an army these Germans have, bringing them hot soup with the last shot! For Christ's sake, what's next!? I've really messed my pants. But for the moment there isn't any more soup men.

We managed to get down and away without meeting anymore Germans. Other things happened, but I can't squeeze out anymore thoughts. I know in time we found what looked like a safe place to sleep, out of sight. We crawled under some rock, face down, shoulder to shoulder. I don't think we fell asleep; it was more like we both passed out exhausted.

Next day, it was real nice for the moment that I woke, but of course that only lasted for the few seconds it took me to remember where we were. Prayerfully, I implored my Dragon to spare me from another day like the past one. Especially after seeing how we finished the day. Look at it! Lordy! We hadn't slept under a ledge, or a crevice, we had been sleeping under a huge boulder just hanging on the side of a cliff. Keeyrist! And I'm still here? What a heart I must have. Still ticking. I think that when I die, they'll have to take it out and beat it to death with a stick!

For the moment we were free again, but surrounded by enemies, virtual prisoners to possibly be caught or killed. But I think my Dragon likes to play with me. And I have no choice but to go along. We're out on like a vast plateau filled with little golden bushes, and even runts of trees, I do believe, if I remember correctly. But now we have a new enemy! An unannounced, undeclared enemy, but an enemy nevertheless. The A-rab; they're like fleas on a corpse. Everywhere.

The first day of this obscene way of life we were in, we had been staggering around, wondering if we were getting away from trouble or perversely getting in deeper. We met some other GIs running away as we were, except they were going in a different direction. They had between them saved two grenades, where we had none. Even so, Solan and I decided to keep going our way; besides, there were five of them, whereas we were only two, and less apt to attract attention.

Later, when we had parted from the five, I found that I had three sugar cubes in one of my pockets from the vile lemonade drink we were issued. We decided to split one each day until we got back. I mean, hell, come on, how far could our army have run? I remember how hard it was to split them evenly; we even took turns licking up the crumbs.

Later that day we allowed ourselves to be smiled and beguiled into an A-rab shack by the promise of food and shelter. They gave us some bread that wasn't bad except it had large lumps of salt in it that were like hard candy to eat. Then, utterly stupid, we both fell asleep, exhausted. Why we weren't killed I'll never know. We awoke at dawn, rested and at peace for the moment, but then, hey, we fortunately wondered, where's the man? That bastard's gone to get the Germans for sure! We took off from there fast.

Groundless suspicion? I don't think so. We had only gone a little ways when I found my wallet was gone from my pocket, with my parents picture and the picture of my 1939 Chevrolet, my pride and joy, the first car to have the gear shift up under the steering wheel. Also a great car for getting girls. Oh, I must close my mind to that; that must have been on a different planet. This one doesn't have girls, calm or even sanity. We had been robbed. Solan's pockets had been picked also. Fortunately for us, the guy who did this evidently didn't have guts enough to cut our throats. I suppose he would rather have gifts from the Germans for turning us in.

Since I knew absolutely nothing would ever make me dive to the bottom of my foxhole in fear again, I knew, not as a promise to myself but in the very seething blood of my body, my reaction to fear or capture would be to strike, if need be with only a rock in hand. That made the A-rab now as threatening to us as any German with a "burp" gun. And must be avoided. This was not overreaction. As was found later, the A-rabs, rotten snake bastards, were found to have killed guys for their boots or what they wore, even using their underwear, burying their bodies in some cactus patch, stripping the dead of any army gear. Later on while fighting in Africa we watched French soldiers going among A-rab huts, and if they found any gear belonging to any soldiers of any army, it was like an assault on your eyes to watch as they would kill all of those in the hut belonging to that group, including the women and children, and even their goats and donkeys. Then burn the hut down. They dealt out a terrible penalty, more than we could ever do. But it was needed to keep these sub-human maggots off our dead.

Two, three or even four days of walking the long way around any open area, and more than a few times running, panting, sobbing, to get away from people and their dogs constantly barking at us. To this day I seldom look at a dog without thinking of the different ways I could kill it; not hurt it, just kill it. Or instead of its mouth, have each bark come out its rectum! Wonder how long they'd bark like that? Yes, you can see I've given the subject some thought. Well, anyway, for the next three or four or maybe five days, I can never remember the exact amount, it seemed forever, we were hounded by the A-rabs with there dogs, horses and even donkeys, and the many sly bastards trying to entice us with food or friendship to come along so they can score with the Germans for turning us in. We both always carried rocks or whatever else we could use to scare them off, these dirty, baggy, would-be captors. In my exhausted sleep, I'd dream of blasting my way back to manhood, blasting every bastard around here keeping me running like a beaten dog. "Son's of bitches! I'm still here!" I'd fervently yell and wake myself. All I could think of with wicked passion was, *If ever I get back here with a tank, I'll grind them all to hell in the ground.*

Solan, God bless him, was my only stabilizing comfort, helping me keep my sanity. Now, here again, I'm in extreme distress, panting, sobbing, laying face down on the ground under some small trees we had crawled under. Again we had run to exhaustion, physically drained by exertion, expecting any second to be shot in the back. This time by an A-rab on a horse with a shotgun. Lying there, teeth clenched, wishing hard, *if only I had my piece*, no words big or small can describe the feelings in my mind; it was ready to explode! That four letter word H-A-T-E was just bursting to strike!

On the last day of our ordeal, I remember well, an A-rab suddenly came upon us riding a horse. A beautiful horse. I didn't know they had such things. What I wouldn't give to get him down off of it! These people had been hounding us all along. They believed the Germans were here to stay. He was carrying a shotgun. He didn't point it at us. He pointed in the direction we were going, saying "Urman, Urman," then pointing all around, "Urman." Then he motioned us to come to him. Solan cursed and threw a rock he had been holding at him. I made a threatening move at him, still holding my rock. He took off and so did we. We knew he was going for help. We ran back, changing our direction. We ran and ran until after some time we flopped down exhausted, exhausted in a way you can only achieve by having your life threatened. You have to believe you're drained of every bit of energy and nothing can move you.

Lying there panting, sobbing, gasping for breath, I thought, *It's not a Dragon that's after me anymore, it's chickens. Damn, stinking A-rab chickens. Lousy chickens everywhere, and I can't do anything to them. Damn the U.S. Army for deserting us. After tearing my life apart, they leave Solan and myself to fend for ourselves.*

Laying there I could feel something in my head changing, roaring. I wanted revenge, to hell with feeling. I didn't want to punch and hurt anymore, I wanted to kill them! Tear them apart! As I write this now, it's hard remembering this terrible self, for I know it went from that to this: Something is interfering, demanding my attention, past the hatred boiling in my mind. What could possibly override that? Listen. Fuzz in my ear. Whatszat, another miracle from the beloved Dragon?! How hard it is not to believe I'm making up a story, because miracles are always hard to believe. It's wild, but it happened. Because next the miracle!

I stopped panting. Listening, I heard it. Stop panting. Hold your breath; listen! I felt it. I, I, I. Listen! My ears perked up. "It can't be, Solan! That's a light tank! An American light tank. Do you hear it?" The tongue-rippling *thrum, thrum, thrum* of a radial engine? No, it's my Dragon! He's purring happily, giving me a break. He's laughing, purring, just like an aircraft engine that's put in our light tanks. I know that sound, the sound I heard for ten weeks training at Fort Knox. It's a light tank, our light tank.

I'm up on my knees. "Solan! Solan! I know that sound." I wanted so hard to believe I was hearing that sound. "Listen! I had to start them so many times! Solan, Solan, get up! Do you hear it? It's ours; it's American. It's down there, over in that gully over there. Get up, come on."

Crawling, we scramble down a bit, cautiously. There it is, on a slight rise off the valley floor, and there's outlying guards with a spider-mounted "fifty" trained on us. We stumbled, crawled, shouted our way down the side of a hill. It was a "First Armored" reconnaissance patrol. A Jeep, half-track and light tank. All weapons were trained on us until it was clear who we were. The lieutenant in charge wanted to know what direction we had been traveling, how many Germans we had seen, etc. We begged for some water. As we got some water and food, being cautioned to eat and drink only a little to avoid cramps, we explained of our escape and what we had seen.

We were welcomed by the lieutenant, who said he could use all the men he could get. I told him I was really a tank driver, trained in the same light tank he was using. I told him that hoping I could get in the tank and go back up the hill to blow some people to hell.

Ignoring my plea, or not listening to it, he said, "That's great, can you drive a half-track?"

I said, "Sure, I'm qualified in that too."

He wanted me to drive the half-track so the guy driving it now could help on the radio. I saw that pleased him, so I asked again, not for the tank, but if first I could just borrow his "forty-five." I wanted to go back up the hill with it stuck in my back and "surrender" to the guy on the horse. And tell him how sorry I was that we threw a rock at him. Oh yeah! I wouldn't kill him, just gut shoot him. And maybe blow away the horse too.

I think the lieutenant could see by the hate in my eyes and the clenched teeth that I wasn't just talking. He said it was all right by him, "but we're not here to fight, only to report. If any Germans show up, you'll be left behind." That cooled me.

Oh yes, how well I remember all this, because I'm the guy who owns the mind all this is spilling out of. How could I ever get to be so mean and bloody-minded? Lord have mercy! Now, of course, I've just passed eighty-five, and I'm a kind, friendly old man. Oh yeah!

The lieutenant continued, explaining that what we were to do was to move forward, that's east, and upon coming to any area where we didn't have a clear view, we'd dismount and go forward on foot. So Solan and I worked in with the other men. I got to drive the half-track and Solan got to ride with the shotgun crew protecting us. The half-track brought up the rear, and when we stopped, my job was to get in the back and protect the rear with a track-mounted fifty.

Far from being scared, I was elated! Whooee! Nothing could have made me happier, except to have some Germans come along to get anointed. Here I'm going, so to speak, from a homeless, defenseless person to king of the road! And a fifty-cal goes with it! A fifty! The very first time they all went off and left me, I didn't feel alone; I felt ecstatic, like the biggest bear in the woods. Remember now, I'm writing about what's going through the mind of one guy standing in the back of a half-track caressing the swivel fifty.

Now I'm back in the Dragon's cage, and he isn't scaring me witless anymore; he's smiling on me. I've been well trained, and I can help feed him. Far from daydreaming, I'm watching sharp.

The lieutenant is back. "Okay, Dave, move it up."

We got to like the outskirts of one of those "dirt plaster" villages. I'm a little distance from, I would say, a four-foot wall. Someone's backyard, I guess. Again the guys went ahead, spreading out, to see what they could find. I'm thinking, *This is like the way Stone Age people lived. Only this must be known as the "mud" age.* Everything is built of dirt clods held together by mud. Even the four-foot wall is the same.

"Yes, sir, Lieutenant. I'll watch sharp!" And I went to the rear with the fifty. I was standing at my post, enjoying the feel of the fifty under my hands, the fifty warmed by the sun. How easily it moved, safety off, caressing the "butterfly" with my thumb. My only thought was that this baby was to take down some Germans, if it killed me. Oh yeah! I was high, high on power! I had it now. Now I'll show them. All that starving, running to exhaustion, fear, humiliation, cursing the army for running off and leaving us, the harassment of the stinking A-rabs, if only I could have gotten to that one with his shotgun and fancy horse.

Now my strength was coming back! Food in my belly, weapon

on my belt. The lieutenant had also provided me with a forty-five. A driver can't very well carry a rifle or carbine in an enclosed vehicle. But where are the Germans? Haven't seen any these past two days.

I would like to interject something here in a way of explaining the following. In my mind at the time was the fact, proven by the events around me, that guys could be dead and wounded by the dozens in the space of a few moments. The war, or the "Dragon" as I thought of it, was loose, and I was in the "cage" where normally he was kept, to protect the human race. In time he was bound to get me, and I was to the point of the mouse daring to fight the cat, knowing he can't but determined to get in a bite. Now, the Dragon I both feared and admired, as it's the indisputable power here on the premises, does the Dragon I speak of seem a little bit clearer to you? Because now the Dragon has provided me with nothing less than an armored vehicle, and a fifty-caliber machine gun loaded with beautiful, shiny brass rounds. Now is my chance to lash out, not for my country, not to be brave, but to get even, to leave my mark before the "cat" gets in his bite.

And now, suddenly, on being elevated from an unarmed fugitive running from all, to the fearsome, armed to the teeth, born-again son of the Dragon that I was, I was going to breathe some fire of my own! This finally is no dream. It's real! Feel it!

I caress the barrel, rub my fingers over the fat brass rounds. This massive weapon is a Fort Knox weapon I trained on. Each time I get up off my driver's seat to go to the rear to be guard, I go quickly, hopefully. I'm all by myself. Far from fear, the only anxiety I ever feel is that I won't get to use the fifty. I hope to see some Germans moving up on us. I want to kill some of them so bad; I have to get even.

After having the German attack deliver me into the hands, wiles and stinking presence of the A-rabs, I feel so besmirched, having my manhood literally pissed on these past few days, I'm almost suicidal. I'm sure I've got to cool it. Just because my body count is way ahead is no reason to ignore caution.

There is one time I remember when I was alone, guarding the rear, and I had stood up on some gear, holding onto the fifty so I could see over a mud wall just to my left. I had hoped to see some Germans sneaking up on me. Oh, what a bath I'd give them. This time I did see a movement. I dropped down quick, anticipating whatever. It's an A-rab on a mule. These A-rabs must be born mean. Look at the size of the little mule, or is it a donkey? The A-rabs toes are dragging in the dirt, raising his feet at times to kick the beast in his hollow ribs. Now here's a guy who's really suicidal. He rides up to a loaded, cocked fifty with a sneer, as if to say, *What, you back?* His right hand is under his rag-bag robe. He must have a piece in his hand. He wouldn't ride up here with such confidence without something to give him guts. He has his eyes fixed on me, not looking at anything else.

I take a quick look around, especially where he has come from, to be sure there are no others; he could be a diversion. I had been tapping the weapon, my scepter, my badge of office, as he came up to keep the barrel on him. What do I look like? Is he crazy? I can't believe he has the balls to ride up to me alone. He's frowning and waving his free arm at me, as though he's chasing flies or bugs or me away. His face is ugly enough without the frown. Looking at me, his jabbering seems to say, *Who are you, and how did you get back? You rotten American, are you all alone? I got something nice for you. It's in my hand. You and your gun are worthless. You think I'm afraid? You're shit! The Germans* (pronounced, Urman), *my friends, will hear of this, and you will be chased away again.* He's mad as hell about something, and loonier than me. What a pair we make.

Now he's looking past me, down either side of me. A tightening of his ugly face gives him away. He's getting ready to shoot; he's going to pull out a pistol and shoot me. I love it, I love it! He couldn't give me a better excuse!

I held up my left hand as though for silence! I was like Moses on the mount, but my right hand was gripping the fifty, cause this might be close. As fierce as I could make it, I laid it on him. Leaning forward, showing my teeth, you loony bastard, my buddy and I suffered five degrading, miserable days of hunger and fear from people like you, you crap head. You hairy, ugly wart. Hiding and running from your kind, fearing being turned over to the Germans. The day-after-day feeling of helpless hate burst through the top of my head. Unclenching my teeth, I bellowed, "Who are you, you miserable bag of shit? And well you look it." I pinned him with my eyes. I knew what I was doing; I was pushing him, urging him to pull the piece on me. "That's close enough! You bastard, stay back! You wanted to shoot, shoot!"

He's changed. I can't really see his eyes very well, they're so dark, but his lips have formed an "ooh." Will he run or pull his weapon? I kept at him. "You wanted an American, you dirty Urman-loving son of a whore. Here I am." Aw shit! I wanted to say more, but I had to move fast. He was shifting his weight to unlimber his arm. And with just my thumb, so easy, I sent him to hell. Him and the mule, and even a chunk of the mud wall behind him, disappeared in a blink. I let out a yell, a howling yell to the heavens, trying to outroar the fifty, trying to punch a hole in the air above me with my fist. Oh, how I love this fifty, my scepter, with it I can stand tall again. I need never run from any man or men again.

Now, as I have said, I like to keep this truthful, and I can't honestly say they were the exact words I spit at him, but they were as close as I can remember.

Immediately the lieutenant was banging on my helmet. "Stop, you'll give away our position!"

I yelled back, my ears still ringing, "What do you think he was going to do?" But he didn't hear me. I saw his mouth say with a hand wave, "Get up front. We can move up now." He didn't even see what I fired at.

I picked up the other guys who had scouted ahead, including Solan. They wanted to know what I fired at. I told them there was an A-rab on a mule looking me over; he had one arm under his robe, and I was so afraid he was going to shoot me I fired first. Solan looked at me. I smiled, big, nodded, thumbs up. He gave me back the prize-fighter double handshake. Great! Getting one of those bastards sure made all the humility and crow we had to eat these past few days go down easier.

After that we did some tip-toeing around, but didn't see any more Germans. Our troops were coming back, and now it was the Germans on the run. After we pulled back to some town or cluster, the lieutenant who had been in charge of the reconnaissance patrol told us we would have to go back to our outfit, as the First Division was here reassembling. We found what was left of Company "A" after asking an MP where we could find our outfit.

Great Christ! I could have bashed the dumb, brainless bastard!

VI   BACK WITH COMPANY "A"

The MP wasn't what you would call subtle. He came right out asking, "Oh, are you a couple of those stragglers?"

"Stragglers!" I blew up, "You son of a bitch." I reached for him, ready to grasp him, knee him and break his jaw with my not-yet-calmed-down helmeted skull. After all we had been through, to be called such a name in such an insulting way in front of others. I howled, "How many Germans have you killed today!" Then, hoping to have him hit me first, I needled him more. "Have you ever fired that weapon on your shoulder at the enemy? You're part of the bastards who ran off and left us."

Solan, God bless him, grabbed me and was holding me back. Assaulting an MP could mean prison time. I was pulling wildly at Solan. I knew what I wanted; no more punches to the ribs would do. From now on it was to hurt, to hurt hard and put down anyone I had cause to attack. (Please note: Today, as a man in his eighties writing of such caustic, murderous feelings, I'm ashamed, and yet I can't be ashamed. That boy, that soldier, had been tormented too many times by the raging, or even at times languid, caressing lips of promised death or dismemberment. In attempting to do the violence in assault or defense that he had done, no slur from a stranger could be tolerated. And this I well remember.)

The guy said (I think), "Take it easy, buddy. I'm sorry. I just got here. The whole division is coming together now. You can bet we'll kick their butt! We're getting more men, heavy guns and tanks."

Tanks? I thought. Now there's something else. Tanks ain't worth a damn if you don't know how to use them. And don't forget the anti-tank guns and tank destroyers. I also had another thought about our little enforced jaunt. Think about it: "News Flash—Green American troops cut and run! From fear." Listen! They got it backwards. Cowards don't run; cowards put up their hands. It takes guts and spirit to run! You could get killed.

Company "A" had been reformed. Now maybe we could get back at some of those Buggers that made us run! Oh yeah!

The best thing that could have happened to Solan and myself was being picked up by that recon outfit. It made me feel like a man again, not a beaten dog being chased by Arabs. Getting even with one, I got to taste blood, real blood. I remember once we were back in the fold, new clothes, underwear, socks, new rifles, grenades, and there was more of those ugly WWI daggers. I didn't hesitate; I put one back on my pants belt like before. Now I was back in business.

The next thing I remember, we were moving through like a small town searching for any Germans and watching for booby traps, and I did that thing you've seen. I believe it was the movie where the soldier opens a door and sees himself in a mirror and blasts it. I did that, but as I jumped back I didn't fire because I saw my American helmet. But I won't go into that; you'll think I added on, which I promised not to do. But, oh hell, I'll leave it in, because I did it long before I saw the movie. So there.

It's no joke clearing houses. From there I believe we relieved some British troops who were defending a large group of British artillery. They had dug like a WWI trench on the front of a small hill, which they manned at night; they fell back to the far side of the hill in daytime. Now at least there were other American units around, but of course I can only speak for Company "A." If the Germans came after the artillery, we were there to stop them. As always, I can't give you specific dates or units other than my own since I never thought of keeping notes. One specific night does stand out as we were in the trench all night expecting an attack. We got a lot of flares, firing and shells, but no attack. But the reason I remember it was the pouring rain. I was standing in the trench with water up to my crotch! No raincoat, I was using that to cover my piece. In the morning everything below my waist was shriveled, and I mean everything! After that I had to tie a string on my penis to find it.

The company was like in a small village, and we, that is Solan and myself, were in a small house with a big porch. Or maybe it was a barn with a shelter outside for whatever. The buildings were all made of like dirt and mud, and even that looked good compared to the insides. It was like when something was built, it was against their religion to ever clean the inside. Why should they? They brought in dogs, fleas, vermin and even donkeys that they slept alongside of to keep warm. You can bet every house we had taken over was given a bath and scrubbed down.

Sitting down, I took off my leggings and boots and was amazed to find I had no socks! Hell, I hadn't been able to take off my boots, never mind the socks. What happened? My sister, God bless her, got the biggest laugh when I told her this story. She was always worried about me and knitted a pair of socks of the finest wool. I remember when I got them and put them on, for they felt so good and gave a little spring to my step. Little did I know I'd be wearing them and my boots, wet and dry, for the next two weeks. So when I took them off all I had was a ring of fuzz just above the ankle of each leg. They looked just like the flowery rings that you see teenage girls wear on their ankles today. That is when they are not wearing jeans. Or how about those knee-high boots? Oh yeah!

Afterwards we were holding a line somewhere and we were taking turns going back at night to the cook's Jeep and trailer to get hot food. It wasn't far. The cooks managed to get their Jeep up pretty close to us. Some, I heard, were killed getting too close! This spot popped into my mind watching *Saving Private Ryan*. Just as the men were asking for Private Ryan, I heard the cooks asking for Dave Lawrie. Hearing my name being called by people I didn't know was kind of freaky. I asked one of the guys dishing out the food, "Did you say 'Lawrie? Dave Lawrie?'"

He said, "Yeah, you know him? He's one of you guys."

"Sure, that's me."

He hollered to the mess sergeant, "Hey, here's Lawrie."

The sergeant said, "Take care of your buddy, eat your chow, get your gear together within an hour and come back here. You're to return to the field train with us."

I asked what's up, and he said, "Are you a driver? All I heard was something about driving. Now get going and report back here to me."

I got the food and stumbled back to Solan. Oh, Christ! It's the tanks. Now they found out I'm in the wrong place. Now, after I've seen what they do to our tanks, you might say I've lost the desire to be in a tank. Now I'm sure I can do, and have done better, with a rifle. On the way I got to thinking, remembering those days not everyone could drive a truck or tank. You didn't just step on the gas; there were gears involved. Once you were tested and passed, it went on your record. How could I get out of that? And at the rate they make tanks "kaput" over here they surely need drivers.

I told Solan what happened and I said, "Don't worry, I'll be back. I'll tell them I have 'closet phobia,' pretending to be stupid. I don't want to fight in no tank—they're nothing but moving targets! You saw what they did to those other tanks. I'll bet most of them didn't get to fire a shot! At least with a rifle I can see what I'm doing. And to shoot at me they have to find me." Oh yeah! And then we parted, giving each other a slap on the back. It wasn't a "good-bye" slap; it was more like a "see you later" slap. Neither knowing we would never see each other again!

I went back to the cooks and was told to climb in the trailer. They had a Jeep and a trailer to distribute the hot food. Now, the trailer was mainly empty and the Jeep was full with the mess sergeant and his crew, so I rode off from "Buddy" Solan in the midst of jugs, containers and whatever. And from what was the most vicious, murderous part ever of my life.

Part of me still feels the emotion as I write this, and another part stops, unbelieving. Could it really have been like that, David? You better believe it! Those nighttime patrols, it wasn't like in the movies, where guys bunch up endlessly talking. That's the movie writer's effort to get everybody in the picture. And no one is ever too tired to talk. For real, a grunt, a nod or a hand signal, that was the conversation. Or take a ten-minute break, flop down anywhere, chin on your bandoleer or the sling of the extra mortar round you carry for the mortar crew, because every round may count! No, there's no idle talk. Keep your piece up close to your body. If you foul it, you'll get only one shot. And that could be bad. Then all too quickly, on your feet! Pass it on, let's go. Yeah, I remember, pick it up, move out, spread out! Always! Spread out. Dead on your feet. Until a burst of adrenaline—Firefight! Jerk up your piece, with a push of your forefinger snap the safety off, an automatic reflex as you get down. What's happening? Give a cupped hand signal to the man ahead, meaning, where? He points his piece. I see. Pull the trigger, pull the trigger. Bastards. Try to see, but keep down. Hell, I forgot to count. Damn, how many rounds have I fired? I've learned, anytime you get a chance to get an extra clip ready in your hand, do it. And be sure to keep it clean. I struggle to get an extra clip in my left hand. I'm panting, feeling. I see some lumps not moving. I'm up on my knees trying for another shot. I've got to stop fighting like this or I'm going to get tagged.Back down, still hugging the ground. No more movement to see. Then guy to my front, fist pumping, pointing past me, means move up, pass it on. Then I fist the guy behind. We got to get going before we get mortared. (I feel aroused; the pencil is filling my mind.) Must have been an enemy patrol. What's left of them has no doubt departed. I hug my piece to me, squeezing it hard as I can to stop the shakes. The hot smell acts as a soother while I caress the stock. Sweating, heart beating. I feel it! Triumph! Triumph! Hey, I'm still here! I'm still here! You bastards! Oh, hell yeah! How many times I got to yell that?

All of these thoughts are going through my head as I bounce around in the back of the trailer. Who would ever think of cooks as brave? If you saw what getting to the "line" under fire was like sometimes, you'd agree. My thoughts were on tanks. After seeing what the enemy could do to them, it was going to be hard not wanting to back off. Thinking in perspective, what's worse, the line company or the tanks? I know what's worse! Guard duty!

Nothing in the war is as responsible and at the same time as hateful as having to stand guard. Standing guard in a line company when your company is facing the enemy was a real test of nerves and courage. You had to understand there was nothing friendly in front of you! Nothing! This means of all the thousands, tens of thousands of GIs in the war, you were at the time the closest to the enemy. Believe me, an unwanted honor. Any enemy patrol would have you in mind, so your first duty was to stay awake. No joke intended. You had to focus your mind not to get your throat slit. Stand by a tree, bush, rock, anything that would break up your silhouette. If you must move, make it low and slow. Looking at your watch can be a torture, for the damn thing doesn't seem to move at all. Ever! Another strain, holding your finger constantly on the side of the trigger guard. Be sharp, don't get trigger happy, you could kill a fellow soldier. But to speak of duty, no duty is greater than protecting the men depending on you, the same as you depend on them.

Then, still bouncing around in the trailer musing, I thought of the upside of guard duty. The upside makes me wax lyrical. If you caught the right shift, you could be rewarded with the most beautiful sight in nature. DAWN. The sky starts to lighten up, the trees appear to be like black grasping veins against a lighting sky while the ground, valleys, trees and whatever stay dark. Your sight begins to sharpen, the vagueness of your surroundings begin to wash away like a semi-opaque curtain is rising with the sun. Your fears begin to evaporate with the morning mist. Vague shapes begin to protrude beyond their covering darkness to reveal their true identities, quieting the mind. The lighter it becomes the lighter the weight of your tension becomes. Ease your finger off the trigger guard, snap on your safety. No enemy can hide in this! Then the brightest golden light in the universe first peeps, then stabs around the side of a hillside. It's the sun itself, the real glory. It appears, revealing itself in the tops of the trees. Truly the hand of God. As it rises with the new day the radiance begins to descend through the branches, and each leaf bursts into golden glory. The entire tree sparkles from every single leaf. The ground itself changes from a dirty brown drab grayness to a dazzling shine, so that even the dirt and rocks come alive! You feel the touch within your body. No matter the war, you have lived for another day, and find the earth abides. Through it all, the earth abides. You feel sure this day will be better! In my belief, and everyone is entitled to his own, I feel the sun is truly the source of all life. Nothing else is comparable.

As an example, here is a memory of something I experienced once on guard, and it took me from the hell and fear of the night to wanting to live and see life again. Because I believe the true aurora of God is revealed to us in the blazing glory of the sun. But because this revelation is daily, its simplicity can't be accepted. But I accept it, and it's my idea, although I understand many Indian tribes worshipped the sun. How can anyone deny my thoughts? In my own way I believe that the blazing shine, the aurora we see and heat we feel, is not God in itself, but it is emanating from whatever form we know, or suppose we know it to be. The radiance is there in plain sight, and it is so brilliant to behold that even those desperately seeking our Lord, our God, our Creator, cannot grasp the true glory it is, and turn to other means, other religions. For myself, when I seek the hand of compassion, care, or acknowledgement of a prayer, especially after a hairy night like the one I've just been through, I position myself to bathe in its brilliance and warmth, and it returns my mind to peace and stability. You doubt me? Then just imagine the day the "glory" doesn't appear.

But now to get back to the bouncing trailer and the thoughts that are running around in my head. I feel someone has unlocked the gate and let me out of the "Dragon's" cage. Could life be worse in the tanks? Once I'm in one of those, as long as I'm alive, I'll have a place to sit. I won't have to tramp all over the land lugging my gear and digging foxholes, but then again I won't have my "blue blanket." You know what keeps kids happy. Rubbing their cheeks. In my case, the butt of my piece against my cheek, hugging it and getting to use it on the "Buggers," comforts me. And again, I won't suffer the many times of being pinned down, unable to see or fire back. But most of all, I don't think I can last much longer in a line company. Hell, Solan and I are among the oldest in the company already! And if I don't keep down more, he'll be the oldest. Now remember, these are my thoughts. Maybe at times confused, but they're my thoughts. Truly, it's a wonder I'm still able to think straight. I've made up my mind! If they want me to go back to the "Armored," I won't fight it. And the clincher to my decision is, I'm sure there will be less standing guard involved.

The cooks dropped me off at a tent full of officers. They had some corporal show me a bunk in one of the tents. He told me to get some shuteye. Man, I have arrived! The next morning, great! What a morning. I had slept on a cot, not on the ground. Now I can write my parents not to worry about the infantry anymore. I'm back where I belong, inside a big steel tank.

After I had chow (breakfast) I reported to a first lieutenant. He explained I was to drive a captain in his small truck. I asked, "A small truck? What's a small truck, a Jeep?"

The officer said, "No, it's a three-quarter-ton Dodge."

I really couldn't believe I wasn't dreaming. Not only was it not tanks, but it was to drive a peanut of a truck! And for a captain yet! Then, wait, I had a thought! I asked, "Most officers ride around in Jeeps; why does the captain need a truck?"

"Well, soldier, you see, sometimes when he visits the companies he takes 'needed supplies' with him."

As I say, I looked at eyes and there sure was a twinkle, but I wasn't pleased. *Naw!* I thought, *I didn't enlist to be some captain's "dog robber."*

Now, here again I must inject some words, because I can't remember the originals. I remember the circumstances. I felt the lieutenant would understand my feelings, telling him I enlisted to fight, not to be in a parade or become some officer's private driver as he went about making social calls. *Bam!* I got a big, "WHAT? Social calls?! Holy hell! Where did you get that? You want to fight? You'll get to fight. You'll get to shit your pants, where he takes you. I've been with him enough times to know! You're a driver, you've got a feisty record, that's why he picked you. He's had enough weak-kneed drivers. Now let me see if your behavior can match your mouth. Let me see you stick with him, and have him tell me you're good! I guarantee he'll test your worth as a soldier!"

Now I hollered, "WHAT? Test me? (I remember this part because privates don't usually yell at lieutenants.) Test me !? I got 'bou cou' Germans to test me . . . and they lost. You think I just got here and have done nothing? There's no way a captain with a little truck can pull out more of my pubic hair than Company "A" did. Endless patrols, firefights, being chased by things I could only describe as Dragons, huge damn tanks. Dragons that we didn't have to fight back with. Dragons we tried to slay with rifles. After sending us up bare ass into Kasserine Pass without enough ammo *or* support. The only way the Buggers got through us was because we had nothing left to fight with. We were left with only our dicks in our hands, so to speak, if you'll pardon the expression. And although my buddy and I got away, we were very bitter to find the U.S. Army had nobody to see that we got more ammunition. You look like a right guy, lieutenant. I hope you'll excuse my bad temper, but you touched a button. Can't really forget being chased like a beaten dog unable to fight back all because of an oversight in providing ammunition."

The lieutenant agreed it must have been a tough time. I saw my chance to get into the lieutenant's good graces, telling him this tough tale. "How about now you tell me what the captain does to frighten all his 'chickens?' You've got me interested."

"He's the regimental ammunition officer. His job is to see that all of our companies have all the munitions they need, at all times."

"Hey! Hey! That would do it. That's the job you want me to do? Drive for him? It's fate, the job that fate has laid on me, to even the score with all them Buggers up in them rocks. Now if what you tell me is true, and that's what the captain does, I'd be a proud and happy drive anywhere, anytime. To supply others, so that no one will ever be left empty and defenseless in the face of a charging enemy as we were. For that I'd do my best and never fail him, never!"

Now, of all the times that I can't remember, it's my first meeting with Captain Kendal. I guess I wasn't that impressed. Let it go. Like I say, I don't like to have to make up stories, but it didn't take long to be reminded this was not Fort Knox!

I really got around. It sure wasn't like the line company, where we got only the bare bones, and even then, only the bones the people didn't want. Anyway, the awakening came soon enough. We didn't take any "needed supplies" to the artillery; that was done mainly by six-by-sixes, not our rugged little buggy. The captain let me call it "my little bomb" and put my Brooklyn flag on the hood.

One of the first trips we made was taking him to an artillery site, where a lot of officers where in a tent. After dropping him off I was told the truck could not stay by the communication tent, to park out in the field. Unknowingly, I went out and parked by one of the big guns. At this particular gun, I believe they were 155s, there was a bright, full-of-pep guy wearing jodhpurs. Now these are the kind of pants you wear when you're wearing full-length boots around horses, and of course, we had no horses around here, and he had no high boots. Just GI shoes. He said he liked wearing them because they didn't flap around his legs. Oh well, everybody is different! After a little talk I got down to the point. Did he have anything to swap? Sure! For a German pistol he'd swap me the Jodhpurs. I laughed. "No, thanks." But among the things he did swap me was a can of purple plumbs. Purple plumbs! After all the crap I had been eating, this was like hitting a jackpot! Cream de la cream.

Now, as I have said before, I can always remember pertinent or overwhelming things. Oh yeah! So what's to remember about purple plumbs? Just then, here comes a Jeep. Another officer! "Soldier, you must not park near the guns!"

I was just outside the edge of the camouflage net covering the big gun, and the guy I was talking to had disappeared. I guess he saw the Jeep coming and popped down in a shelter. The officer said, "Pull over by the trees."

Here again (I know I'm talking stupid, but it's the way my brain has been rearranged), looking back I think of it as one of the many, endless times the Dragon's tail, so to speak, bumped me to the side to get me out of the way. Cause if I had stayed . . .

I got over to the trees, salivating about the plumbs, and I was just getting out my miniature can opener. This was the work of a genius, this little piece of equipment about an inch and a quarter long and half an inch wide when folded, and shaped like an inverted figure seven when open. Placed on a can's edge to use as a fulcrum, it easily opened the container. Some people at home really helped with their efforts to equip us with the best, and they did it from this tiny can opener to the huge artillery pieces in front of me. Well, that certainly was quite a dissertation on my beautiful little companion, the can opener that I could drop in my pocket as part of my "equipment." Aw, sheet. Hell's fire! The forty millimeters, the anti-aircraft weapons, had started with there *Poom, Poom, Pooms*.

Drop the can and out of the truck! Run over a ways, away from the truck; it could be a target. Get under a tree. It can protect me from the scrap falling from the AA guns, and I can get the trunk of the tree, hopefully, between me and them shoot-em-up black crosses.

Expecting to see the bastards zooming over the hill, guns blazing as usual, I was amazed to see for the first time, just like in the newsreels, they were coming out of the sky, like tied together by a string, riding down an imaginary railroad track. Oh, Mother! Dive bombers! But I wasn't watching a newsreel! I was right under them. I don't know if I was shouting or not, but I was hoping the AA would hit one of these guys. How could they miss, coming down in the same piece of the sky? Oh baby, the sound is overwhelming. It's going to be close.

I did my thing, digging my fingers and mouth into the dirt. How can you describe this feeling of tasting the last moment of your life? It's like laying in the road knowing you still have a chance if the elephant's legs miss you. Oh yeah! This was different! I still heard the whizzing, cracking, snap of bullets, but not expecting the slam of the five-hundred-pound bombs nearby, feeling the shock lifting into my stomach. It really pounded the ground. That's what made me think of being in the way of elephants. I know other guys had sillier thoughts than that, plus filling their pants. With me it was always different. When the "Dragon" held me by the short hair, breathing in my face, making my skin crawl, I was always in a rage, fighting to keep myself down. Let me get up! Let me get up! I'll shoot the shit out of them. But now just a few shots left.

When it got quiet, as it always does eventually, there was nothing to shoot at. My rage always seemed to run up and down inside of me with nowhere to go. I would shake and get sick, trying not to show it. Just look at the place. There's my truck, but the dust and dirt is still hanging in the air.

As always, there was screaming howling and moans. I sure missed Solan, the squeeze of his hand on my neck or the friendly punch in the arm with, "It's okay, Dave." Together we gave each other courage. Now here I am without him, thinking I had a "tit" job, but those bastards with their black crosses are still after me. With no companion, no strength from another, I've got to fight the shakes off myself, gotta find the captain.

I'm shaking. I'm out in the open. It appears everything's all clear from the sky. Me and the truck were out of it. Nothing came close, but Christ, look at the mess of those nets and guns! Those Buggers really tore them up. Men and ambulances were all running around. My only thought was to get over to that tent where I left the captain. Oh no! Where's the tent? Everything's a mess over here. But luckily the officers had had a special trench dug for their use. The captain was okay.

I don't remember all the details, but we got dirty helping out. Medics were working over the wounded; the dead were put to one side, laid side by side like on the beach. And pieces to sort out by the "graves registration." And there was one there that had jodhpurs on the leg. Maybe it had been another kid, I couldn't tell.

Afterwards, getting in the vehicle with the captain, I guess he could see I was upset. I hadn't mentioned the momentary friend I had made. And it was his quick death that upset me. Christ, a laughing, joking kid one minute, and bam. Next some poor mom will get a telegram. I'm mumbling, "I'll make it up for him. Not those double-damned black crosses that I couldn't get at, but some Bugger somewhere."

The captain started talking to me, telling me not to worry, that I could never be hurt while I was with him driving his little bomb. Because that's what it was. Of course, he never called it that. It was like we were forever loading up with 60mm mortar packed in containers, three together. I just said, sure, that was great! You can bet I'd never be hurt! If anything, and there were plenty of anythings to ignite in that truck, we'd only leave a hole in the ground.

At night, going right up to where they were firing, it was very important to keep the lowest silhouette possible, so that the only high point on the truck was the spare and the top of the steering wheel. The tire was handy in a way; anytime I had to bail out, I would flip off the ignition switch and vault over it. I had suggested to give me more room by leaving it off, but the Captain said no, it might be needed some day. "It might be needed some day." Again, another twitch of the Dragon's tail. I heard his hot, hoarse voice whisper, metaphysically of course, "He means for you, dummy, not the truck!" But of course I don't believe stuff like that.

A short time after that, it was pitch dark and I was carefully following the tops of the telephone poles that could be seen against the sky, alternating with watching the difference of the road against the edge of the road to get up to wherever we had to go, when like a bolt out of the dark a Jeep going far too fast for the conditions just missed a head-on with us, and ripped into the side of the truck, gouging out half of that big heavy tire. All I got was a shock and a bruised arm from being slammed against the inner part of the tire rack.

We took the two men who had been riding in the Jeep farther up the road to get first aid. But it was easy to see that without the tire, the Jeep would have torn out a very big piece of me! "Captain," I said, "it was lucky we kept that tire on there." I believe the captain said something like, "You don't need luck when you're with me, Dave. You'll be okay." That's a nice thing to say, but it seemed to be a silly thing to say. But of course I hadn't really had enough time to get to know the dedicated and determined man the captain was. And as I found out later, he was fearless to the point of driving his other "sick" driver to want out.

Now, it may sound like big talk, but after what I had been through in the line company, anything we did with the truck could never match that! I was on gravy train. Better still, we would be delivering lots of goodies, like mortars, 30-cal and 50-cal grenades, and whatever to put down lots of those German Buggers. Oh yeah! Now if only we could declare war on the A-rabs. Grrr. And in time I got to know the captain, real well. It got to the point where we meant as much to each other as Solan and I had. He had pulled me to safety at the risk of his own life when I couldn't move, and like Solan, he never showed any fear. Of course, that doesn't necessarily mean he was brave. It could also mean he was dull-witted too. No, he was too smart for that, just say "stupid too." Now, now! Remember, ignorant is when you don't know any better; stupid is when you *do* know better but do it anyway!

Sometime later we visited another artillery site. I had just pulled away after dropping the captain off. This time I pulled off to where I had seen the mess (kitchen). A good place to try to swap and stay far from the guns. But then I saw the captain waving me back. He was with a chaplain. I'm not in favor of chaplains. A pretty nurse could help a man's spirit better. Oh yeah!

I was to take the chaplain wherever he wanted to go. He gave me and the truck a blessing, then told me to go around behind a row of tents. Some guys back there put a box on the back of my truck. Now remember, the truck was just flat and open; I could see everything. The chaplain was blessing the box. I thought, these guys bless everything. The box was the size of a box (in the States) that they put lettuce in. A wooden box with wire straps, and I would say it could hold at the most half a man. I could see there was blood on it. When he got back in I asked what happened. He said they had some counter-battery fire in their last position last night. I said, "I'm sorry. Is that all they found of him?"

"Oh, no!" the chaplain said. "That's all they found of the three men."

Now, on my honor, I'm not laying it on you, It wasn't a man, or two men, it was three men! That's what he told me, and that's what we had. The three guys had been in a small trench they used for cover, and from what the others could see afterward, a shell must have landed in it or on the side of it. The trench was gone, leaving only a crater. What had been found of the men was all they could find among the dirt and stones.

He took me to graves registration, where they off-loaded the box. The chaplain was staying and told me I could go on back. I got to the captain and took him back to where we had been camped. And then found out I wasn't going to sleep in the back of the truck that night. Maggots and blood! The tailgate and truck bed were covered with what looked like nine million maggots. UGH! I took a five-gallon Jerry can of gasoline and sloshed it all over, hoping that whatever these tiny horrors came from, they would be back home by morning! The hell of war came in many shapes! Oh yeah! (Please note: If some of these "memories" seem redundant, it's because I don't write in sequence. I wrote almost all of it as it came to me, spelling and thinking as I went along!)

Another Day

It was one of those days that later in life gave me a strip of gray hair across the top of my head. It was about one or two inches wide above my right ear. It really was that big and that white. I had by then made it to age twenty-three, was home and was married. My wife called it my German hair. And you know, I think she got it right. But let's get back. Now I had another buddy, a real through the sweats buddy, even though this time he was a captain and I was, as always, a private. We went through a lot together: the fears, the shakes, the great feelings of accomplishment. He was Captain Kendal, Regimental Ammunition Officer, First Battalion, Twenty-Sixth Infantry Regiment, First Division. And I was his driver.

The captain's assignment was to keep all of the regiment's companies up to regulation in all types of ammunition. Caring for the companies in reserve was easy; the companies on the line, under fire, were not! Sometimes at night guides would lead through the darkness with something white. My sweat was that they might miss a mine or a hole; their sweat was that in the dark I didn't run over them. But the captain said that if the cooks could get up to the guys with hot chow, we could get up there too! With whatever they needed to kill more Germans. He was not only dedicated, but fearless. He told me he would never be killed! What do they call that? Famous last words. But what the hey! It was better than wondering when our little ammo truck would blow a hole in the ground.

On this particular day we had just came through the usual dump of a town called El Guetar. The guys in mockery called it "El Banjo." Another pile of dirt and plaster houses. This one had some stores in it. This is where I got my German swastika flag. I can't recall the details, but I remember the steps in front and inside of the store were all made of wood. I guess I remember this because it was so unusual. There was an odd uniformed guy there ahead of me taking down a German flag. He turned out to be a "correspondent." I told him I was looking to get one of those flags. Then he said he already had one and I could have that one. I tried to reciprocate by offering him a Walther German pistol or a Beretta, an Italian one, but he said he was looking for a German mess kit set. I said, "You got it. I have one out in the truck." He came out with me, and as I gave it to him he saw my Brooklyn flag on the truck and laughed. He said half of the army seemed to come from Brooklyn and the other half from Texas. I still have both flags (German and Brooklyn). The only links I have to the past, these I managed to get through the hospitals. They stole everything else before I got the flags home.

Well to get back! As we drove through the outskirts of El Guetar, there was a beautiful sight. Guns, big ones, tanks and tank destroyers, not these pop guns that had been mounted on half-tracks but real killers, 90mms mounted on fast new tank chassis. Now, there was a piece of equipment any man would be proud to fight with. They could really do the job! Oh, Mother, those Germans were really going to be paid back in spades! And for their planes, nice new 90mm anti-aircraft babies, not 40mm weapons mounted on towed four-wheeled carts! USA! USA! Sorry, I'm just proud! Standing up proud! To look at all this new equipment and all the new men, American men, it gives you the ability to fear nothing. If they shell us, our equipment will pinpoint their position, then our counter fire will lay on them what they have laid on us without fear of response. You actually hope these Black Cross planes will show up. These nice new 90mm guns and the forked tail fighters with the white stars will blow them out of the sky. From now on most of the planes we see will have the American white star or the British bull's eye. Now a man can throw out his chest and say, "Bring it On!"

Now again to get back to "Another Day" (this tale). As we came out of the trees into like a long valley with streaks of wadis (ditches) running in our direction, the ground was like rolling hills, and this donkey wagon road we had to take had white tape all along the north side, telling you that side had not been cleared of mines, something I had learned not to take lightly. The captain tapped my leg to get my attention. Our little code: Tap on the arm: Stop! Rough shove: Jump! I nodded, oh yeah! Because only a few days before we had a very close call with a mine. And when it was over and I said how lucky we were, the captain said, "No, Dave! If you believe I have a good fairy, you and I will live forever!" I turned to laugh, but his eyes caught me. They weren't crinkled as with a laugh; they were somber, meaning what he had said, he meant! I have to wonder if he ever made it to the age of eighty-five also.

I had developed a trick one of my uncles had taught me about fighting, fists that is. Look at the other guy's eyes if you can. If you see fear, no problem; if you see determination, brace yourself. In the captain's eyes there was no joke. Just a plain, simple statement of fact. Just like today; look at President Bush when he speaks. No movement of the eyes, no up, down or sideways look, no wavering of the eyes while talking. Believe it when he says he's going to bust ass. Just hope it's not yours, Iran!

The captain had told me before about never being killed. But he had never mentioned a fairy. Some guys had godfathers or angels or those black beads, but I never heard a man claim a fairy. Well, since a private can't, or will wish he hadn't, razz a captain, I let it go. I was interested to see how far it could go. But to me what had happened to us on an easy daytime run up to the "line" guys was luck. The "big hole in the ground," "end of the world" luck.

Our three-quarter-ton, four-wheel-drive Dodge truck had by rough calculation at least two tons of mortar and a few other odds and ends aboard when we came up to a "dead" German tank that sat broadside to the road. Now, you have to use your imagination whenever I refer to a "road;" there were some macadam roads, but only on the main routes. This one was dirt. We had been going around the obstruction of the burned out tank for a couple of days. Each time I went around it I thought of the story of the tank. When it was hit it was hit in the side, and its fuel and engine started to burn. The crew had been shot down as they tried to run. Then a man started screaming, trapped inside. Then the same men who had shot down the crew in one of those incomprehensible acts of war tried to save the guy by putting a rope around him tied to a Jeep, but only succeeded in pulling his body out, with only the flesh of his legs attached. Leg bones remained trapped. I'm not telling this story just to dish up some "glop." Its important to understand that my thinking of this, looking at the burned-out tank, distracted me enough to let one of those big engineer trucks cut in front of me. I only had time to start a curse, when with a huge explosion the front of the engineer lifted in the air as it was blown apart. And in only the space of a second, down came all the pieces—mud and rocks splattering on me as I gasped at all the crap I was trying to avoid by climbing up in my helmet. (Mentally, a guy can climb up in his helmet.)

The captain had another officer beside him. This officer had a peculiarity of never wearing a helmet; he hated them. In all of this garbage that came down on us, a rock about the size of a large watermelon had crushed a five gallon "Jerry" can in the outboard carrier right alongside of him. It had missed him, but not his imagination. In spite of his fellow officers' teasing, he never again went without a helmet, although we all knew a helmet could never have saved his skull from that rock.

I had a death grip on the steering wheel, and my foot was trying to push the brake pedal through the floor. Looking to my left, I saw the big spare tire and reached for it like an old friend to help pull myself up. Standing in my seat to see ahead, holy hell, what's next? Sure I was shaking, why not? To stop the shakes I yelled my yell: "I'm still here! I'm still here, you bastards! Next Bugger I get a bead on, I'll shoot him twice." Then I laughed, looking at the mess of the two officers, forgetting I looked the same. The laugh had stopped short when I saw the rock that the other officer almost got to wear and I pointed it out. Now my shakes were gone and the captain's friend had them. I knew then I'd have to get another gas can, and the other officer must have thought, I have to get a helmet! And he did, but only after his fellow officers teased him about locking the barn door late. Oh, before I forget, the three men riding in the cab of the engineer truck climbed down, dazed but unhurt.

An engineer truck is built much heaver and stronger than an ordinary 6 x 6. Some guys they say are blessed, but not, I hope, the Buggers on the patrol that planted the mine. You may notice I don't use words like "Heinie," "Krout" or "Jerry." They have no feeling for me. I say "Bugger" the same as I spell: HATE. Now that's got feeling! I get wet, hungry, scared, exhausted, sleepless, screaming meemies and knowing, really, I'm doing terrible things, all because of some people named "German." Now here, just for the matter of luck (or the captain's "fairy"), if we had gone first I wouldn't be standing here. And I want to keep standing here as long as I can, standing on top of as many of them as I can! Hey now, don't forget I'm giving you insight to a twenty-year-old mind sixty years ago. I'm really very nice and lovable today!

Now to get back. I'm sure it was a double mine that had that much power. And if we had gone first, our little bomb would have added to the story of the tank. You know, the burned out tank sitting on the edge of that big hole! The captain's good fairy was directing traffic that morning. I'm intrigued; its fascinating. I'm beginning to become a true believer. It helps to be a believer. I guess that's what religion is all about. I've told this little story so you could understand my state of mind as I drove alongside of that white tape now.

I really feared and hated the tape and the lousy mines. Double-damn them. When you see pieces of still-screaming men blown up in the trees, you can understand the evil force that they are. A mine is a crummy way to get it; I always hoped if I had to die, I'd do it pulling a trigger. That's not big talk; that's the honest reading out of my mind. That chance now seems gone; driving the little bomb leaves very little chance of using a rifle again. But this is its only downside. Hey, look at the upside; all of those rounds of mortar, grenades, the tens of thousands of rounds of fifty- and thirty-caliber cartridges I delivered had to be doing more than I could ever do with a rifle.

As we went up the road, I was happy and proud to see the growing might and muscle of the U.S. Army. And the fact that, as small as the captain and myself and our little stripped truck were, we counted.

We had been back to pick up ammo for the First Battalion companies that were out on the line. We had mainly mortar 60s and 80s in clusters of three, small arms, grenades, etc., and I could feel we were overloaded. We came up to a Sherman that had parked too far from the bank on its right side, so I couldn't get between it and the tape on its left. The captain stood up and hollered to some guy sitting on the edge of the turret with his feet inside. "You have to pull up, so we can get by."

The guy looked bored, and hollered back, "F--- you. You can drive over a little of the tape."

I was just about to holler back, "You're talking to a captain," but the captain spoke right up and said, "I've got over two ton of mortar on this vehicle. If I go up, you go up!"

I laughed to myself, because the captain was bluffing. Remember? We would never be killed! The guy dropped back inside, then with some rattling and groaning the beast pulled farther up the road, and I got by, without touching the damn tape.

We started up the grade, with the captain standing watching ahead, and also the road. Sometimes you could spot a mine by a depression in the road. When a hole was dug to plant a mine, you couldn't very well pack the dirt back in too hard; you might kill yourself. So eventually this dirt would form a depression. Be alert!

Looking at him, I admired him. He stood like Washington must have stood in his boat. His job was to see that every company in our regiment was up to regulation in ordinance. And when the need was urgent, which was usual (What else?!), we would load up our little ammo truck no matter when and get it up to them. I say "little" ammo truck because everything is relative. It really wasn't that small, but since the only thing it was bigger than was a Jeep, you could call it small. Compared to all the large and mighty vehicles around us we were small, but like an adder in the flock is small. We carried the real juice. Look out! And that's the reason it was used. You couldn't get a full-size truck up to the line without bringing down attention due to its size and noise. The three-quarter Dodge was perfect for the job. It hummed more than it groaned. It was geared so low that if you got on a smooth road like the macadam it always felt like it wanted to go to another higher gear, which it didn't have. It was stripped, no side boards, no windshield, and of course no cab or lights. The only thing that stuck up was the top of the big spare and the top of the steering wheel.

I'm sorry. I'm off again. To get back to the road, it was all bushes, rocks and that always present Cactus. These were big; the needles were about three inches long and the tips were like fire, the tips that got you at night if you weren't careful. We were told they contained poison, and if you walked into one, you could believe it. It felt like red hot and biting needles. Anytime I could run one over with the truck I did! I wanted to kill it. Seems I got to the point of wanting to kill anything, except a fellow soldier, since being in Company "A" with a rifle, learning to use it with fervor, doing it with the courage my father had given me, telling me I was a Scotchman. "If you have to fight, fight with one thing in mind. Get one of the Buggers before they get you! If you do, laddie, you'll not be wasted. And if you get more, you're ahead. You can't lose."

Yes, sir! Easy as that. You can't plan it, but it happens. Scared out of my wits, but doing it. And as always, with the last few shots after any action I feel my pulse trying to burst out of my temple, my teeth locked together. "You didn't get me, you bastards! You didn't get me," I shout, I howl, for relief! "I'm still here! I'm still here, you bastards!" The stupid shaking, the urge to piss. Oh, hell, I guess I laid it out for you before. But I'm wasting my breath. You can never understand. The force in my brain to get one more before I'm got.

And now the "Dragon" has put me in charge of a small truck that can deliver more death and destruction than my little rifle could in a hundred years!

And now if only I can stick to the story, "El Guetar," I'll try to fill in some more about our moving the tank. We were going up the road, and of course this was no "Sunday" drive. As we worked our way up the pass, we had to watch everything carefully. We were between the rear area and the "line," where anything can happen and happen fast. This particular drive I'm reliving as I write. Up on the crest we were approaching, we saw two guys in the road. One guy raised his rifle over his head, a signal motioning us on. The captain waved back. "Hey, Dave, there's the guides." No sooner had he said that than thunder struck. I saw them both dive, not jump, but dive off the road. Not a friendly move! Hell! They're Buggers, and they've got a heavy weapon just over the crest of the road about to blast the truck! I flipped off the ignition and started to vault over the big spare. Planes! What?! Who would ever? Jeez! Directly over the road, hugging the crest, same as when I was in the infantry. Not again!

Being so distracted, I fell flat on my face and chest, knowing I had no chance. Good-bye, Mother! Falling flat from the top of the spare knocked the wind out of my lungs. They felt crushed. I couldn't even gasp. I couldn't lift my face out of the dirt. I don't know how many guns and cannons those planes carry. But these planes seemed the loudest! Hammering at the back of my head, and yet I felt nothing strike me. All I could do was press my face into the ground, thinking this is impossible. Prone and clutching, a gale of dirt blew against my face and even up my helmet, leaving me spitting. In the rush of air, "How can they keep missing?"

Then in my wild mind it dawned on me. Of course, they're after the bigger fish we just passed through in the valley. All the tanks, half-tracks, guns and guys. And then, right in front of the roaring, fire-breathing, lead-spitting Dragon, the captain rose up, exposing himself, pulling me into the hole he was in. It wasn't a hole; it was a gun pit, empty of a weapon. The captain kept helping me, dragging me to the near side, the side against the heavy firing from the valley. The planes were still roaring right over our heads, with the blasting cannon and ripping machine guns over the howling of their engines.

The ground was jumping from all the hits around us, but that was from the heavy stuff (tanks, half-tracks) we had just passed through firing at the planes. I wasn't cool, calm and collected this time. I felt like one of those elephants I talked about before had squashed me a little. Looking up, I realized the captain was covering me with his body. Oh, man! What the hell next?! I guess if he thinks I'm acting like a child, he'll treat me like one. But I'm not acting, I fell!

Then, as always, eventually the firing stopped. I got up and had to relieve myself, leaning against and over the wall of the pit that was only three feet high, I guess. I was filling my hands with dirt, squeezing it fervently; the inside of my body was churning. Looking over the parapet I could see the familiar sight of ranks and vehicles below burning and several explosions scattering fire into the smoke, and with the last few stutters of AA all was quiet. I really missed the relief I got from firing at, or back at, something. You may wonder how I can remember and write about these things; it baffles me. I'm sure I could never remember all this unless I was concentrating on my pencil putting this down. The pencil is the trick; it scratches the ever-hardening crust of a dimming memory. And through the scratches, vistas of a very violent few months. And as these forgotten memories emerge, I sometimes think, oh yeah! And then sometimes I think, oh no!

I clearly remember lying prone on the ground, looking over my shoulder, gasping for breath after smashing to the ground, flat on my chest. Seeing the captain rising up out of the pit, pulling me in. Bullets, dirt, rocks, shrapnel, churning the air. He was risking his own life to save mine. Later on when I thanked the captain for risking his life to save me, I'll never forget what he said. He said, "Dave, how could I be risking my life when I've told you I can't be killed!" I want to change that phrase, famous last words, to famous lasting words.

We still hadn't gotten the truck up the hill. Now, I'm sure my mouth opened, I know my eyes opened! There was that miracle truck; it hadn't been touched! Well, not completely. What I mean is that it hadn't blown. But the evidence of its surviving one hell of a gale of fire was on it; it was plastered with dirt, brush and pieces of cardboard torn from the containers holding the motor shells. I could see it had a few new scars, but at least the tires were still up. I'd say it was sitting not twelve feet from where we had been huddled. (That's two spread-out arm lengths.) If an explosive had hit just right, it sure would have deepened our pit, and us with it.

The two "guides" I thought had been Buggers came down the road to us, telling us how lucky we were stopping where we had because so-called friendly fire had torn up the top of the hill. The guides climbed on board. Sitting on top of, as I have said, over two tons of dirty mortar cases. It didn't bother them. I guess they were part of the crew that was to used the stuff.

They told us to go up to the crest where we had seen them, follow the turn to the left, then just a little way down to a rag on a bush, and turn off to the right through the bush downhill. When we got to the top, the road was more like a wide dirt path, where part of the hillside had been cut out to make space for the path. Up against the wall of the cut was an extended pile of bodies—Italian bodies, bodies in odd positions, no weapons, no helmets, crunched up or spread-eagle, arms flung out, pockets emptied, personal belongings scattered about, the usual pictures of women and children, loved ones. The captain touched my arm. The signal to stop.

We got out to look; the bodies were already swarming with maggots. Now please, you can skip this. This is not pleasant. My pencil has reached way under the rug. I can't remember the last time I ever thought of this. But I'm pledged to tell the truth and I won't cover up for any "sick" fellow soldiers. I walked along the row of bodies, hand on my forty-five; this is how tensed up this had gotten me. Looking up and around, I didn't know what to expect! I could feel the hair on my neck, the shrinking of my eyes. The bodies, all Italian, had been defiled. Maggots where the ears had been, swarming in the pits of the eyes. One man's mouth was stretched wide open, swarming with maggots. Looking inside, that's all I could see. Another's pants had been pulled open and his crotch filled with the same living, swarming, mini white monsters. Bastards! Bastards! Who could have done such a thing?

I heard the captain raising his voice to the guides, something he seldom ever did. They said they had seen them there yesterday, mostly covered in blood, and believed the Rangers who had been ahead of them had done it.

What had made me tense and clench my teeth as I approached was the hope I wouldn't see what I knew I'd see. Someone had lined up a bunch of easy-going, always-ready-to-surrender Italians and murdered them. The Italians were not cowards. They simply did not want to fight Americans. And what was on my mind? Me! Imagine! If they had done this, and Italians knew of it before I walked in front of that machine gun, "Surrender!" they would have cut me to pieces. And if the Italians spread word of this, no more easy surrenders. Some of our men would have to die to take them. All because of this!

I can only add to this story of the "brave" Rangers that most if not all of them were caught in a trap in Italy. A fake spy had led the battalion up a "secret" gully to get behind the Germans lines. The Germans had lined up both sides of the gully with men and heavy weapons, and when the rangers were beyond retreat, they opened up, killing half and causing the other half to eat crow by putting up their hands. That is not a rumor, but a fact! In the history books. Amen.

My pencil has failed me. I can't remember the rest or going back. All that emotion tearing at my mind. And the inability to change anything left me disgusted. But after that, going back down, I do remember seeing the guy in the turret who had moved his Sherman for us cleaning his fifty. I gave him a big thumb up, happy to see a fighting man fighting fit and cleaning his scepter after surviving the black-cross planes, giving me the pride and pleasure I always get seeing another American soldier. Oh well, I'm cooled off.

When we got back to El Guetar we made camp there, and that also reminds me that the road to there is where the Jeep smashed into the truck. By the way, the two men in the Jeep had been a little banged up and had been given a lecture by the captain. And wherever they went, I don't know. Now, El Guetar was where they placed a lot of large 155mm artillery pieces, and they fired in daylight, out in the open, not in the trees. They had a lot of camouflage mounted on poles over the pieces. At night, the Germans came in bombing, not where the guns were but in the trees where we were. Seven days and six nights, this is where I was sure I was going to depart this "vale of tears." Where we were was like the opposite of what they called "hedgerows" in France. Here in Africa the Arabs for irrigation had dug these deep ditches. I'd say approximately four feet wide by six feet deep. This was great! No foxholes to dig. Ready-made latrines. This was the most secure area we had ever been in. Oh yeah! Remember what I just said about the 155mm? They harassed the Germans during the day, and the Germans retaliated at night by bombing where they *thought* the guns were. And this could really make a man wet his pants, because you could hear it and see it coming. Even so, in all this shooting and bombing we had only lost one man. He, no doubt, had flipped under the strain and had gotten up and ran down the road, something that all of us at times wanted to do. I beat this feeling by digging my fingers into the dirt.

One night in frustration I climbed up a mud wall that was a side of one of the ditches and emptied a full clip (twenty rounds) from a B.A.R. into the side of a "flying pencil," the nickname of a German plane that was built very thin and long and carried bombs. I felt I could do this because I noted how close they flew to the tops of the trees. From our position you could see them diving down on their approach, kissing the trees. Now, I always wanted to try to "give it back." But this was to prove to be a poor idea. I had loaded my "clip" with alternate, ball, armour and tracer. Now, maybe because it sounds like a "brag" I shouldn't tell it, but I did it, so I'll tell it. It was the first time I ever fired at a plane. And I thought I had a good chance; my line of tracers seemed to hit the body just behind the wing. But before I could see any more, a bomb hit just on the other side of the wall. The shrapnel was absorbed by the mud wall, but the blast blew me backward into the bottom of the ditch. A guy already taking cover down there asked me if I was hurt? I said, "Nah!, but I'll bet I put some brown in the pilot's pants!"

He got after me, one of the company's sergeants. He said, "That wasn't brave; what you did was stupid! The luck of your hitting the plane is minor. But the plane and its bombs hitting you is like 95 percent to 5. Really dumb odds."

I told him my purpose was not to be brave. I was just damn mad at those dumb Germans flying directly over the guns they're after and dropping the bombs on us. I know I took a chance, but it made me feel good. That is, until he dropped the bomb. I thought then I'd have to find a better way. And besides, I'm still here! I'm still here! No, I didn't shoot the plane down. It just ignored me! Oh yeah!

Another night, whistles blowing; damn sakes, here we go again! Now, I may sound festive writing like this, but that would be false festivity. When you hear the hum way off, but coming closer, and nearby guns start to fire, you know what's coming. Run, take cover, get down in the hole, all the way down. Get up in your helmet, and stick it in a corner. Oh yeah! They're going to test the strength of your scrotum again. Press your body against the dirt in the hole. And then, WOW, you're born again. You hear them flying off.

Now, one particular night I headed for one of the ditches that I new was clean. Just as I was about to jump in I saw the shape of another man jump into one of the very unclean ones. I hollered, too late of course, "Hey, Mack, that's a latrine!"

A very loud voice came back. "I know it, soldier!"

Jeez, the battalion commander? I know his voice; I hope he doesn't know mine.

We were using the El Guettar area as our base. From here we could run back to the "field train," load up, then get it up to the companies. You might say we were in the middle or between our points of necessity. This is where we ate and slept. We hadn't moved this base recently because the companies were being held up by Germans fighting, doggedly, fighting not to give ground. Again after another bombing attack I was climbing out of one of the pits and I saw what looked like someone had lit a small cooking fire. Holy hell! What's that? One of the 6 x 6's had been parked away from the tents because it had a full load of gasoline "jerry cans." I ran over and saw the engine, or the truck's own gas, had been set on fire. But to my chagrin I feel my memory pulling tricks on me. As sure as I remember this happening, a real "hair raiser," a beacon to more Buggers bombs, or a very big blast if it got to the load, I can't remember how we got it out. Since I limit myself to not making up stories, I have to leave that blank. But not the fear of the moment. Maybe it will come to me later. I feel I had to run off to do something else. It would have been a smart thing for me to do. As I'm writing now, it occurs to me how we put the fire out. We took our helmets and used them like shovels, scooping dirt and sand up to throw on the fire to put it out. Whew! Oh yeah!

In all this time, seven nights and six days, only one man had been killed. In one of the attacks he had gotten up and ran. No doubt he had seen a better cover "over there." This is one of the real tests of "soldiering." If you're caught out in the open, get down, hug the dirt, and stay down. You will always see a better spot or imagine it. The sudden urge to piss or defecate. A true brain-busting urge to get up and run trying to break your force of will. But real soldiers, that is, experienced men, know that shrapnel sprays outward, and unless the shell lands on you, you have a good chance of being missed. I was amazed watching the movie *Band of Brothers* to see that anytime they caught shells or mortars they're running around like replacements, yelling, "Over here, George!" or "Get up and run over here; it's better over here." I know it's only a movie. It better be. Oh yeah! Remember, when the shit hits the fan, take cover and stay there!

Another thing I'd like to insert here is that I always felt if I were to be killed, I wanted to be killed fighting another man, not by a stinking mine, shell or bomb. Now, of course, in my eighties, as the sports like to say, "I choose to be killed by a jealous husband." Word of honor, the following is not a brag or complaint: I never prayed. If God put me here to be tested, how can he test me if he's helping me? No! My way home is to strike down before I'm struck. Or is it stricken? Scotchmen are right. When there's no chance, at least try to make it even. It's very hard to think that way now, but when your "in it," your genes uncover power both physical and mental you never knew you had. You're revved up to maximum adrenaline. For the moment, you're "King Kong, The Mighty Dragon Slayer!" You can jump a six-foot fence! For the moment! Then it leaves you just as quick, shaken, insides churning. How many times can you do that? Now again you can feel your tongue is sticking out as you put the piece to your eye and start squeezing off rounds. We're off again. On the Dragon's back! No ride can be more exhilarating or more fearful. Now! Now! Put it to them! Fire! Fire! Scream, yell, keep squeezing, squeezing, squeezing the trigger. What's the Dragon doing? I feel that fiery breath hissing past my ears, and I see the bloody claws tearing up the earth in front of me. Crap that's flying is trying to blind me. Now's a lull, a few more scattered shots. Now falling back exhausted. Amid all the death and destruction. Yell! Shout! Get it out. I'm still here! I'm still here! And I'll do it again! Oh yeah!

What can I say? I'm sorry I did it again. I can avoid lying, but I can't seem to avoid preaching (instructing). At last we were breaking free of El Guetar. Our vehicle was in a convoy moving up; the Germans were being pushed back nearer and nearer to the Mediterranean. I was really feeling great! Hey, General Rommel, how do you like my big brothers? And I've got more! Men and guns, big guns. Scores of tanks and tank destroyers with 90mms to take out your 88mms. Even new 90mm anti-aircraft weapons we should have had before sending us against your Panzer divisions. Best of all, now we've got a fighting general, General Patton. You know what he told us? When we lick them here, we're going after the Hun where he lives, and dig him out! Something else I read that he did when he took over, he called one of the his generals over and asked him, "Where's your foxhole?" Imagine, a general yet! When the general showed him, he went over, unbuttoned his fly, and pissed in it. He said, "You can't do much to the enemy hiding in that," saying the same that I did, unknowingly, when I flipped out in Kasserine claiming I could fight better up on my knees. Unfortunately, losing your head will cost you, eventually. That's why, since I really don't want to get killed, I'm glad they took me out of the line and put me in the captain's truck. Rommel, count your boys!

Just remembering how I felt carried me off again. I am trying to stick to my sojourn. To get back to our moving, we were being guided into a field where sections of it had been cleared of mines. I'm following behind another three-quarter-ton Dodge just like mine, except it had a canvas cover in place, when again, *Whoom!,* right in front of me as he turned his right rear wheel and went over a mine the engineers must have missed, being in a hurry. The truck's load of barrack bags erupted through the top of the canvas cover. I was amazed. Truck canvas is so tough I never thought anything could be blown through it. Then from my usual stance (how many times can I do this?), gripping the steering wheel and trying to push the brake pedal through the floor, I saw what looked like one of the bags moving. So did the captain and the other officer riding with us. They both jumped out to help whoever it was struggling in that pile. I had to stay where I was until guys with those frying pans on sticks (mine detectors) decided it was safe to go around. Even so, it was real goosey driving until I got to my assigned spot. The reason I remembered this was because it destroyed my past reassurance that following in the tire marks of a vehicle ahead made it safe for me as well. I forgot mines went off by pressure, so that Jeeps or lightly loaded vehicles could pass over safely, but not heavily loaded vehicles like mine. And good-bye, Mother!

Damn, damn, damn, how I hated mines and the people who deployed them! The only one time I got involved with one was to help save a guy who lost his legs. Later the captain told me that the very lucky guy that flew through the roof was shook up but still in one piece. He had been sleeping on top of the barrack bags inside the truck. Luckily the full force of the blast had been directly under the axel of the wheel, and the wooden bench and barrack bags above that had saved him. But still, how he could be blown through that very tough canvas and live was a miracle.

Now, the good news was that from then on the First Infantry Division would always stay together, fighting together, just the way it had been planed. We got held up again at a place called "Hill 609" a number I've never forgotten and always steer clear of. This was the last real tough battle we were in. In Africa I say "we." Actually, my job, and the captain's as well, was only running up to this hell of a place with mainly mortar. The area was all slate rock, impossible to dig a foxhole, and building a shelter around your foxhole was even worse because a near miss would send the rocks and slate flying into you. Again death has many, many ways. Bodies and pieces of bodies all over the slate rock. The Germans had picked another tough place for us to fight. But as bad as it was for us, the Germans suffered more. It wasn't easy, it took a lot of ammo, but we beat their best. I didn't get in any more shots. But I was happy, proud happy, knowing none of our guys ever lacked the ammo they needed, as we had in Kasserine. In my mind I had dedicated myself to never having anyone depending on me go without it while I was still alive. Yeah, I know, big talk! Sure, but the feeling of despair in firing a last shot I wouldn't wish on anyone.

Nighttime was always easy; well' not really easy, but a lot easier than those hairy daytime trips. One time, well, I guess I should leave some things out. But then again, if I leave things out you lose the mental vision of what's occurring. Crawling on this damn slate rock, pushing a mortar cluster ahead of me, an American helmet was in my way. As I reached to grab it to throw it aside, I saw it was covered with flies. I thought, *Oh, Christ, I hope no guy's head is inside.* Happily it wasn't; no head, but some kind of gooey junk was plastered inside, and the flies were laying eggs in it. I really hated flies. You had to keep brushing them off and be sure to blow on your spoon or fork to get them off before you put it in your mouth and swallowed. Even so, I'm sure I swallowed a few. While I'm at it, I'll describe a type of fly we encountered in Sicily. We called them parachute flies. They could always be found around the latrines waiting for someone to make a turd, then they would fly in and ride it down! Oh yeah!

VII

Another day, but today not a typical one. This time I had to make a run up to the line with some 60mms and whatever. This time by myself. That gave me cause to easily remember. I think we were getting a little carefree because of the Germans constantly pulling back, it seemed, as I had always been sure would happen. The endless amount of ships unloading endless amounts of fighting equipment was beginning to tip the scales in our favor, driving the Germans up against the wall. It was a situation like when you've heard of Bigfoot, the monster with four-foot feet and two-foot hands, and you say, "Ah, come on, there's no such thing!" It was the same with me when I heard of "Tiger" tanks but had never seen one. So like the guy stepping out of his cabin and coming face to face with Bigfoot, I got to see my first Tiger full in the face.

It was still daylight. I got to a point or bend in the road so that I couldn't see what was ahead. And anyway, by this time I should have come up to the company guides. I hadn't seen anyone. So I got out and went ahead on foot (slowly), making my way a little in from the road (maybe "worn dirt path" would be better) to check. Who knows, I might have already passed the guides, and if not careful would be talking to some Germans next. I had my .45 Thomson with me, cocked, safety off, finger alongside the trigger guard, ready for anything. Its weight gave me assurance. Being "just" behind the line was always a hairy place. And I was ready. Oh yeah!

I can't describe exactly my surroundings, but what I walked into is one of my strongest memories. That is, anyway, up until that time. Moving ahead, eyes mainly on the ground watching for you know what (mines), I stepped into like an opening between some brush and a tree. In this small opening was an oddly shaped old shack. An old shack! Holy love a duck! My eyes focused. It wasn't a shack. It was Bigfoot, my Bigfoot! I found myself and my tiny Thomson facing a tank so big I hadn't seen it. And suddenly, bare-assed, fully exposed in front of the biggest tank and gun that no exaggeration could fit, my Thomson felt like a wet noodle. The tracks alone must be two feet wide, and the cannon reaching almost over my head.

Zip! Behind the tree, back against it, I slid down on my butt. I was panting, my heart pounding, trying to hold my breath so that I couldn't be heard. You know, as I write this, I again feel the outrage. I learned to make two outcries in my war. One was, "I'm still here! I'm still here, you bastards! (I got to yell that every so often.) The other was, "Jeez! What's next, for Christ's sake! And that's the one that fit here. For the first time ever, I wanted to quit. I've had enough! What kind of war is this? The enemy has all the biggest and newest stuff, and we have odds and ends left over from World War I. Squatting under the tree I remember thinking, *What luck. If I hadn't gotten out to scout I'd have driven right in front of this*. Just one of the many thoughts running through my head. I'm sure another was, *Good-bye, Mother*.

The tank didn't have any markings on it; it was all black. Now that was odd. But it damn sure wasn't American. It sure was quiet! All I could hear was the ever-lasting grumble of guns in the distance. I had to do something. I did what gets people killed; I got curious. Hugging the Thomson, I leaned around the tree like the proverbial mouse peeking at the sleeping cat. Well, anyway, not to drag this out any further, the "cat" wasn't sleeping. It was dead! I saw the turret hatch cover was open and a side portal for loading shells was ajar. No live tank would ever move like that. I searched around it. But not in it; I had to remember I was alone. If any enemy found me I'd be a dead duck. I found a hole in its side about the size I could put my thumb into. What did that? I backed away. *You bastard, scaring the hell out of me*.

I was back by the trees when I got that feeling, a feeling I could taste of something I really wanted to do, only this time it wasn't a man, it was a dead tank. Looking around, feeling I was in a world of just me and the tank, oh yeah!, I let out a yell, "You don't scare me, you son of a bitch!" I fired a burst into the side of it. Holy jeez! The noise of the Thomson and the force of it staggered me back; it caught me offguard. I had never fired a Thomson before. My nerves were on end, and some of my brains came back. I thought, *I'd better get the hell out of here before I attract some attention I don't want!*

Getting back to the truck, I turned it around and went back. Going back a way I saw that I had continued up instead of bearing left. Don't really remember this part of it so well, but I had missed a marker and I would have eventually driven into the lap of some Germans and would never have seen the tank except for the fact that the Germans had abandoned it as they were retreating. Anyway, I got to my guides and was told later that it (the tank) had been knocked out by a "bazooka," something new to me, but something to be happy about. If it could knock out a monster like this, then they should replace every M1 rifle with a bazooka! Beautiful, really beautiful! I went from wanting to go home to wanting to go after them! Oh yeah! But again, not to show how smart I iz. (I really love that "Maul" expression. It's something that popped in my head one day; I've never read it anywhere.)

Nope, haven't lied yet! Even the dumb trick with the tank, I did it! Another thing, I really do have a lot of foreskin in thinking ahead. Right now it's happiness, yes, but what's on the flip side of happiness? In my mind I reasoned that if the Germans also had a handheld weapon like that, Oh, Mother! Oh yeah!

An odd thing—when you're not too busy trying not to get killed; when things allow you to concentrate, say, at half speed, you might say, allowing you to operate at peripheral vision speed, you can notice things you brushed past before. When you're in a line company you don't get to see the amount of death and destruction you leave behind as you move ahead. People backing up the line—the medics, artillery and guys like myself bringing up more ammo, cooks with their hot chow—go through it, feeling at times very lucky they missed this or that bloody mess. Still, everyone must always be on their guard, because right behind the line, many times you may be alone, or with only a few other guys. Be sure you keep every piece clean, loaded and ready to go. Enemy patrols are always possible. (Buggers laying mines!) The area aptly named "Indian country." Oh, sorry, yes,

I love our new language; I mean "Native American Country." Hey, Chief Bloody Nose, you native American? Yup! We no longer live in swamp. Now live in wetland, much nicer. Oh, man, sorry, went off again. Writing sometimes is fun, even when the subject isn't.

Lately (now imagine I'm speaking to you sixty years ago) things seem to be letting up a little. And things don't seem to be torn up so bad. I do believe, as I have worked hard at it, I've earned the title "soldier." But even though the pressure is off, the sight of a coal scuttle helmet still sets my teeth on edge, and I'm awash in the thoughts of what I want to do. And even though I can taste it, like with the A-rab, they're prisoners now, and I must cool it. It's not easy standing alongside the men, or men just like them, who just recently were trying their best to kill me and not feel the prickle on your forehead, or back of your neck. Prisoners, getting to see more prisoners now. Some of them just babble and smile, others try to look tough. Oh yeah! What a laugh!

Now, the next particular morning, all was quiet. Quiet in a way I had lost memory of. No blippity blips of small arms, no rumbling of heavy stuff in the distance, no planes overhead or whistles blowing for them after a month or more of incessant disorder. And each awaking, whenever, after getting some sleep and finding, "I'm still here!" And what the hell's bells is next?! And for a change the captain says, "Good morning, Dave!" And he's smiling! We have arrived! Oh yeah!

Yeah, now you know the war's over; over for now, anyhow, but we got a long way to go. The word is out; we're going to see sunny Italy. We're forming up a convoy of trucks. We're leaving this putrid sand, flea and cactus-filled rectum of the planet. It's amazing. Every living thing here is vile or wicked; even the plants have barbs and stinging needles, not to mention the assorted reptiles. Also, flies come in a scale, from the invisible (pinhead) to the horsefly (Ow! Ow! Ow!) This abomination of land that the Jews and A-rabs still fight for possession of to this very day. God must really have been putting his only son to the test to put him down in the most inhospitable part of the world. The inverse of California, this endless, sand, cactus, fly and scorpion-filled hell-to-live-in land, even in peacetime. Peace? That's the one thing they never seem to suffer from here. Hey! Maybe that's it! Hell isn't down there or over there, it's here! Think of it, hell is here, right here on earth, and the biggest joke of all, each of us is allowed to make our own hell. Think of it! I have proof. Like my joining the army—misery. See, like joggers perpetually grimacing as they flog themselves—misery, or mountain climbers as they pull out their fingernails or guts—misery, or how about weight lifters with their distorted faces? Don't forget the skinny girls suffering hunger, refusing to eat. Maybe I'm onto something. Maybe I should start a new religion. Maybe those crazy A-rabs have it right, to pray and pray and pray six times or more a day until they get the permissive impulse in their "program" to blow themselves up and return to the everlasting land of virgins. Wow! That's wild. I just heard (just a note, 2005) that the A-rabs were asked to lay off the bombing for a while. They're running out of virgins. Har, har.

The word has quickly spread around that the war in Africa is over! The Buggers have surrendered. It's weird; you can move standing straight up. No sound to tighten your guts. Now everything is peaceful. Now the shoe is on the other foot. Now it's the German Army shortchanging its men like we had been, left like virtual orphans for supplies and men. Now Patton is our leader, a fighting general. Not the "desk" generals like Eisenhower, who had made us patsies for the British. Now the stuff from home is pouring in, guns, tanks, planes, you name it. And even, thank the good Lord, better food. C-rations are forgotten; now we have K-rations, whatever that means. Who cares? The better food comes in its little wax, impregnated boxes that you can tear up, put in a pile, and they will burn with enough heat to heat a canteen cup of instant coffee or chocolate, or a finger. Be sure <u>not</u> to hold the handle of the cup with your bare hand while you do this or you'll drop it or fling it in the air! Enjoy. That shows people back home are thinking. Superlatives, man, that's living!

Unfortunately there's always a downside. We must remember, a somber memory; we can't forget all those mattress covers we leave behind. They give reason to our determination that our enemies must and will pay! And future good will come of it.

Oh my! Another look back. My pencil is always taking me off on a side trip. Oh yeah! Now to get back to my, shall we call it, observations? The surrendered Germans were being herded together for eventual shipment to the USA or Canada. Knowing that they were safe, the wise guys among them who could speak English rubbed it in to us that they were going for a rest in our land and would enjoy themselves until we got sense enough to stop fighting the eventual "glorious" victory of Germany, and give up, belly up, like the French. Look how nice Germany is to them. For the moment I didn't speak, causing the wise-guy look in his eyes to turn to a "whas" look. Grrrr, if I could only throw one punch. My mind searching for a rejoinder, got it! If my fist won't do it, maybe my tongue will. "That's your tough shit, buddy. We ain't French. Sure, you Bugger, enjoy yourself for now, because by the time you ever do go home, all you'll find is a hole in the ground that us guys have been using for a latrine!"

Mean? You might say so. What else could I do? We weren't allowed to shoot them anymore. Not even punch them.

We finally left them and Tunisia behind us, and our convoy was heading back to the city of Algiers. We had stopped on the way for a noon break, K-rations and a little rest. We had been crossing over the Atlas Mountains, nothing to compare to where I live today in 2007. That's in the Rocky Mountains around Salt Lake City. Now, who would ever have bet on that in 1943? Hey, isn't that a gas? 2007! With that longevity claim I have, you could believe my writing is fiction. Imagine! A nineteen-year-old kid going from a normal upbringing to a, no exaggeration, complete reversal of life. A kid turned inside out after being recently suckled on a witch's tit. A German witch, complete with mines, screaming me-me's (rockets), tanks and planes. Bugger of hell.

Another time, to show how young men converted to soldiers can become so callous and laugh at another's pain because it's not theirs, we were suddenly startled by a loud explosion. It turned out that an A-rab and his mule had triggered a mine! Now, wasn't that too bad. When we all had stopped laughing we started our convoy again, heading over the Atlas Mountains for Algeria, where we were to rest, relax, and train with new equipment. Then on to invade Italy, where our welcome was sure to be more, should I say, "hostile" than it had been here. I have mixed feelings about the Italians. How can I shoot them when their buddies on the machine gun let me live? Well now, you might say, how about the German, that coal skuttle who didn't shoot me when his weapon was right on my belly? That's different, because I feel Germans are trying to kill me every day!

A note: To be honest, I found out some time after the war, just a paragraph somewhere in an article, that I actually owed my life to General Rommel. It said that, in fighting the British in Africa, he had been conducting, if you'll pardon the expression, a "gentleman's" war. That means, I understand, no shooting of prisoners. Those were his orders. And thank God for the strict German Army, for I had technically, at the moment in front of that wild-eyed, frothing-at-the-mouth German, been an unarmed prisoner. And following his orders, my captor, mad as hell with hate blowing out of his eyes and mouth, on didn't shoot. Believe me, I had to read that paragraph several times. Oh yeah!

To get back, driving in an open truck like mine, any men riding in a vehicle without a canvas cover overhead always had to wear goggles because of the flying beetles. They fly everywhere. They're black, as big as the end of my thumb and hard as a rock. More than one guy suffered a black eye. Even one hitting your forehead felt like being whacked with a stone.

Eventually we pulled into Algiers. At first it looked crummy, the dreary, endless shit of the poor people. You know it's only a thought, but it is a thought: God must have hated the poor, he made them so poor. A-rabs everywhere. But as we went in farther to the center, where the French lived, it began to look more modern. Then I saw trolley cars, which of course reminded me of Brooklyn. But this in no way was Brooklyn. (You know why the baseball team of Brooklyn was called the Dodgers? The borough had so many trolly car lines people were forever "dodging" them.) Then, as we got to our camping area, it was fairly nice. The road was divided like they have in Paris, with big trees and flowers on each side. We were put up in some houses; best of all, new clothes, underwear and socks.

I tried to hustle as many pairs of socks as I could. Memories of washing stinking, filthy socks in water at times almost as dirty as the socks—good drinking water couldn't be used for laundry—often, dirty or not, it was the best I could do. Also I remembered the time taking off my boots after wearing them for some time, and the dirty, crappy socks looked like something an unshod werewolf had been wearing.

In time we got passes to go into the "big" town. Everywhere we went the kids were begging "bisquek," which we were told meant candy, and they would try to hustle a cigarette for "papa." Or, "Hey, Joe, come see my sister. She's nice." The guys with passes were provided with truck service to the center of town, and I forget, but we had a certain time to return or be charged AWOL. I somehow, someway still have a pass to Algeria, along with my two flags I saved to bring home, reminding me of the warriors' code, "Kill the men, screw the women."

On the way in, guys were talking about this real fancy house they had heard of and were going to visit, and I made up my mind I would too! And here I visited my first house of ill repute. To feel my oats, first time, and as I keep saying, telling the truth isn't always easy! It was a big building, about six or eight stories high with an entrance like a tunnel leading to the center of it, where we were told we would find a "rotunda." I had never heard of one, let alone seen one. I couldn't wait to see it; also, don't forget, all the girls, we were told, filled it. Oh baby! Standing in a line, backs to the wall, leaving room for others to pass, mainly women, we gradually moved along the wall of this tunnel toward the center. Suddenly one of the women stopped, looked at me and said a lot of gibberish in French. All I did was smile, trying to look pleasant. Then, without any warning, she grabbed me by the balls. My automatic response was to flick a right to her jaw, and even though at the last instant I pulled the punch, she went down. Aw! All the guys said, "Why'ja do dat?!" I really couldn't help it, it was purely a reflex, automatic, and if you don't believe me, go ahead, stand in front of me and try it. I'll demonstrate.

If I remember, the guys helped her up and she was spitting a lot of bad French words at me. Oh yeah! One thing I'm sure of, next time she grabs a guy, she will duck!

When we got inside the rotunda, I was amazed. I wasn't disappointed. I never expected to see such a building in a place like Africa. It was all glass up to the top floor, with glass elevators spaced around. This woman—I call her a woman because she must have been about twenty-five, out of my class, and no matter what I had been through

I was still only twenty, and although I knew many ways to flex my muscles, I didn't know how to flex much else—she took my hand and we went up on an elevator. When we got up there, I stopped to look around and she pulled me into a room and began to teach me tricks. Looking over on her dresser, I saw a fancy picture frame with a severe-looking French officer staring out. Sign language and crappy English told me it was her husband. Oh, wow! Now you're talkin'! Whooee! What could make this more enjoyable? Hey, Dad (in my mind I always talked to my Dad), look at me! Am I a true fighting Scott now? Screw the women and kill the men! That's what you said. Glorious! War does have its rewards at times.

But of course, good, bad or indifferent, nothing lasts forever. I got back down and caught one of the trucks going back, thinking when I got back I should see someone in Medical to get a treatment. I didn't want to wind up like one of those guys with huge blue and purple balls they showed us during an induction film. Remember! Always use a condom, soldier! It was to be my last experience in Africa. Next day, off to the piers.

As I said before, this was one of those times I come up a little blank. There's nothing much to remember about the trip on the ship; it really was very short. I don't even remember the ship's name. Everything was so placid; I think this was because the last day aboard was, like they say, "a night to remember," and part of the day, too! Whatever word fits the opposite of placid, that's it. The last twenty-four hours on that ship stands out, like opening the big double doors to a new madhouse, with the placid ride on the ship coming to an abrupt end when it ran into a sudden violent storm, catapulting me into a nonstop effort of doing my best, giving me the memory of the wildest, maddest, unending thirty eight days and nights of my life. Bombs, bullets, mines, Christ!

But I'm ahead of myself. Let's go back. We went down by the piers or railroads and loaded up with munitions and loads of three-sided sixty-millimeter mortar cases, fifty- and thirty-calibrator boxes and cans and what all else. We tied it down with my camouflage cover. Now, when I say "we," I mean the captain and me. He knew just what extras he would need when he went in with the first men going ashore, and I'd also be with them. But he had to be on a different ship, one holding headquarters, I believe he said. I would be on more of a freighter type of ship that didn't carry any kind of troops, only necessary army personnel. The personnel I speak of are the many, many other men besides me who are involved in this effort, all with similar duties on their minds. Of course the assault troops would hit the beach first, way before any large loads of extra ammo could be brought in. Our small loads would be right behind them, so that made my job very necessary. "Get that load to Blue Beach, Dave!"

When we split, he waved, "See ya on blue beach!"

"Yes, sir, Captain."

I went to the piers, and an officer chalked a number on me, I mean on the truck, and as they loaded other vehicles on board, mine, or should I say, "our" beloved "bomb" went up and on board last. Yeah? Last! Your ass! I won't be going ashore in anyone's shadow! My little bomb wound up near the top of the hatch. I guess for the sake of the ship.

The good thing I remember about this ship was that it was American, with American food. The bad thing was that it was loaded with American kid sailors who stole from each other, playing endlessly like they were at recess. Second time I found my barracks bag open and searched, I taped a note on the bulkhead: "If you're caught, you'll be shot." It's really true, the U.S. Navy takes kids that would never be allowed in the army. No, I didn't shoot any, but I understand in 2007 approximately one thousand WWII vets are dying a day. I predict the last one to die will have been a sailor who enlisted at the age of sixteen. Or maybe fifteen! How about thirteen? Oh yeah!

Now, here is a day that starts out real nice. Army life isn't all bad, especially when you're on a big ship, on a big sea, and you've just finished a big meal. This is an invasion ship. It's loaded mainly with very large trucks and equipment, oversized cranes and bulldozers, and any dangerous cargo (that's me) is stored near the top deck. It has no facility for troops, and we have been given cots to sleep on by our equipment. Since there are very few soldiers on board, we get treated like guests by the sailors. And they allow us the freedom of the ship. Except, of course, the pilot house.

I'm sitting on the hatch of the forward cargo hold, not quite like the couple in *Titanic* but still near enough to the bow to get quite a ride as the ship rocks and rolls along. The crisp, clear air enhances the sight of all the ships plowing along with us. Not everyone gets a ride like this. No amusement park could ever fit in this baby. I'm riding on a ten- or twelve-thousand-ton horse. To give you a better idea of my feelings, I'd like to include some words I found in a book entitled *The Sicily Campaign*. The author writes from a ship in our convoy, maybe ours, I don't know, the following quote:

> It was the hour of twilight on July ninth, 1943, and I stood with legs spread apart on the swaying deck of the "U.S.S. Barnett" and looked out across the Mediterranean. My eyes filled with the dark mass of frothing water, its sibilant, surging swells, the soaring green waves, flecked white at the summits, the sea ahead of me was an undulating, dappled path where heavy transports, dripping and rolling, chased one another in a wavering battle column. On the rest of the sea, thousands of warships of the British and American navies, swaying in sinuous and menacing lines, ploughed deeply through the water and showed now their spray-clouded masts. The air was lashed in a kind of wildness. The noises of the sea and sky were humming as if they would break out at any moment into a violent uncontrollable roar.

I stand abashed. Now that's real writing, writing that's beyond me, because that was really the way it was. The reason I included it is that he can really make you "feel" what's going on. And then to see, almost as predicted, what was a lily pond suddenly become a roaring, heaving "Dragon" trying to get at you. In a way it's really a shame when you're part of something as big as this and you don't really appreciate being in it. You think of it more like doing another day's work. Only, of course, at this job you don't get fired for making mistakes; you get killed! As they say, in the course of human events, it's great to be one of the few who change events, and it's even better if you come out alive. Just think, we were to be the first guys to invade the European continent *ever* from America.

On our quest of "worldly pacification," in WWI it was "over the top," and in WWII it was "hit the beach," neither a longevity sport.

Oh, lord love a duck, I've gone off again. Well, anyway, it's hard not to think like that.

Now, as I have said, we were sitting forward, enjoying the ride. Sailors were busy getting ready for the morning. In the early morning we'd be landing. We watched as they hung one of the big landing barges over the side of the ship with rope bumpers for protection. It was the biggest landing barge I had seen, with armaments of its own, two fifty-calibers, one on each side. The ship had more barges like it, and smaller ones too, all lashed to the tops of the hatches. I guessed the one over the side was the start of getting ready for tomorrow's dawn.

Those big words, "exhilarating," "undulating," I quoted before, we were enjoying them all. Great to be alive! Alive! Sure, there will be plenty of death tomorrow, but not today; it's too nice. Oh yeah! I stood on the deck, legs spread, as the guy said, bracing myself with my arms as the ship easily took the rolling seas, giving me a better ride than anything I ever had at Coney Island. The very large landing barge now and then bumped the padding they had put between it and the ship, but mostly just swayed with the ship.

A sailor suddenly popped out on the small deck of the barge, hopped over to the ship and went "aft." That's ship talk; means rear of ship. I moved closer to the rail of the ship to see the size of this barge, and I guessed they wouldn't put my small ammo truck in that. It was way too big. It even had its own artillery. I mean, on the barge. Two fifty-caliber machine guns. The front ramp that comes down as it goes up on the beach had open work at the very top. I guessed that could let in bullets and shrapnel, but it had to be to extend the ramp and still allow the coxswain. (Isn't that a word, "coxswain?") I guess it has to be something bigger for the guy to be called a pilot. Well, anyway, the coxswain, pilot, whatever has to be able to see ahead. But I made a mental note to get forward under the protection of the ramp if ever I were to get on a barge like this.

You see, I'd been acclimated to the sound of the shell, with its piano-like crashing spewing shards of cleverly designed bits of shrapnel, the sucking sound of a rapidly approaching shell, the whipping snap and crack of a bullet, someone trying to tag you. They all mean one thing—instant respect to the religion we all live by. Get in a hole, like they say, get prone, and like the comedians among us will say, bow! Get down, and when you do, get your head down, way down between your knees as far as you can; that's so you can kiss your ass good-bye. Well, anyway, that's what went through my head looking at that barge, and I'm sorry again, I went off. But my pencil reminds me one must look ahead.

I saw the sailor coming back. He was dirty, but a fine-looking man, carrying some tools in his hand. I guessed he was busy; nevertheless I asked if I could go down with him to see the engine and other gear—I always like to see how things are put together—and maybe give him a hand. But he said, "No, no, sorry, but I've got to get this ready to go, and you'd only be in my way. There's not enough room." I was going to say, "You can always use a third hand," but he wasn't looking at me anymore, wiggling back down the hatch.

Oh well, anyway, it's too nice out here. Who cares? I was back talking to the others. The others were all like me, drivers of some important or necessary equipment. I can't say how long it was, but then so easy, but so hard, the sea changed, like we hit a wall; it felt like the ship came to a sudden stop! A very big wave, biggest wave ever, hit the side of the ship, like in the middle of one of our bounces up and down. We were suddenly knocked sideways. The water didn't come across the deck, but flew up in the air up the side of the ship. Incredibly, the big landing barge was lifted straight up. The front, the ramp, the bow end, whatever, broke loose, pivoting on its stern hook, dropping down, jerking the engine end, or aft end, off the hook that was holding it. Then the whole thing dropped straight into the sea without the slightest struggle or splash. That's not possible! I'm disbelieving my eyes. I'm not writing what I imagined happened or what someone told me happened. I was looking at it. Something that big, to fly in the air, then disappear!

The ship calmed down a little and I staggered over to the railing, looking back at our wake to see if any of it was floating, but there was nothing. All that was left of that huge barge was some broken electric wires whipping around, and nothing else! I got that same feeling again many years later looking at the space where the twin towers had collapsed. Tell me how can you describe that? An enhanced nightmare come alive!

My first thought was to holler, "Man overboard," but two things damped that—he would never get out that small hole with the water rushing in, and orders were, no ship was allowed to stop for a man overboard. The poor guy working inside the barge, he wouldn't have a chance.

Crewmen ran over asking us if we saw what happened, asking about their buddy. Then, all this talking about him reminded me of me! If he hadn't turned down my offer to help, if he had said, "Sure, come aboard," we surely would have spent eternity together, dying like rats in a flooded sewer. This time I could only whisper to myself, "I'm still here! Love of God, I'm still here! Oh yeah, Dragon, you bastard, we're not even there yet and you're pulling my short hairs out. The Dragon, that ethereal, ever-present Dragon, had popped out of the sea and snatched a life.

Afterward, the weather got very bad. Everything on the ship had to be tied down. I had to get all my gear together and double-check the water proofing on the engine of the truck. Funny, I never gave the truck a name. I guess I thought the Brooklyn flag on the hood was enough.

The next for-sure memory was stepping out on deck in the dark from the ship's mess. They fed us a real good breakfast. Since there were way more sailors on board than soldiers, we got treated real good. Stepping out on deck, I got to see the huge lights from shore moving around, then suddenly lighting up the ship. They were firing at us; you could hear stuff howl through the air. We weren't firing back. Or I don't think we were; we were just caught in these big search lights. Fortunately they didn't last long. I'm sure the battlewagons shot them out. The ship's hatches were open; they were getting ready to unload us. The shore looked a long ways away. I went back inside. I never wanted to dig a foxhole so bad in my life.

Now! Now the speakers with there everlasting "Now hear this" ordering all equipment drivers out on deck. I went back out on deck from the mess. They were starting to load the barges that were coming alongside, each man watching for his vehicle to come up and go over the side after it. A black guy, a cook, came out, stood beside me and made a funny. He said, "Man, the sun ain't coming up today, it's being blown up." Oh yeah!

It was full dawn, but no sun yet. The memory, it's spilling out a lot here. I was told I'd be in the second wave. I thought, "Good! The first always gets the worst." But when the first wave went in it was black dark. Now, like the black guy said, the second wave was going in, in the blown up sunshine. Oh yeah! The sun was just peeping over the tops of the mountains, lighting up everything. There! Here comes my four-wheel bomb, and over the side I go! Hold tight to that rope net. If you fall you'll be crushed or drowned. I'm going to go through this next part without erasing anything as I put it down, as it comes to me. If I can. As soon as I landed on like a little catwalk running all alongside of the barge, I had to hold on tight because he pulled away from the ship right away. I carefully worked my way back to the control deck or whatever you call it. There was a sailor standing next to a pedestal mounting a fifty-caliber machine gun that was useless, as it was bent way over, the barrel pointing to the water. They must have come under the counter of the ship to crush it like that. But that didn't bother the sailor; he was waving a forty-five at the sky. The next guy was the coxswain inside a four-sided splinter shield. The third sailor was swinging his fifty around on its pedestal that was in good shape. I was hanging on to the splinter shield looking around and especially ahead. I was trying to see what the shore looked like. I remember the wet, cool water and the splashing air playing on my face as I squinted ahead. The shore was still dark. I was aware this time that this would not go down as a day's work! This time I was surely a part of a very big piece of history. First assault on Europe from America, with not only the sights but also the sounds tearing at the nerves.

I asked the coxswain if he knew where he was to take me. He said, "Blue Beach." Right! That's where I was to go. Then I had to ask, "How do you know where it is?"

He pointed to a part of the shore that made all the rest seem quiet. Columns of smoke, explosions, fire, whatever, being blown into the air. Of course, I should have known! Oh, Mother! Oh yeah!

I would like to interject a word here about my thoughts. After all, that is what this saga is all about. Looking at the violence of Blue Beach I had the greatest urge to tell a lie. After all, it might save my life. I felt like a man in a canoe being paddled ashore to where a huge bear is tearing things apart and just waiting for me. I understand that many people, when they fear they're about to be killed, have their lives flash in front of them. That isn't exactly what I experienced. But I could in a way hear my father's voice, and heard again that phrase, "Act like a man." Remember, if you want others to respect and acknowledge your "manhood" you must keep a goal in mind. To fear "naught" and be known as to never lie, or steal from another. And since I thought of my father as the man I wanted to be, above any of my uncles, my mother's brothers, who were terrific, I decided I would do my best to please my father. Always from then on his voice guided my words and deeds. Very many times, it wasn't easy. But, oh, did I ever want to lie just now. I wanted to say, "Look, just this side of it is where I have to go. Why not drop me there and I won't have to drive around?"

The coxswain said no. "I have to follow orders. Now you better get below and be ready for when I drop the ramp."

Damn sakes, I thought, *I'm going to be killed, and the Germans won't even know I was here!* Believe me, it took all the guts I had to climb down by myself into what I thought to be my dark bouncing tomb! *Jesus sakes, Solan, I hope you're doing better than me!* I can feel the rough cleated deck beneath my feet. I'm on the bottom of the barge; a few staggering steps take me over to the truck. Holding on to it. The "bomb" sits pretty good, being so heavy. I work around to the right side, avoiding the large spare on the left so I can get up into the seat. The truck seems to be shivering and shaking, mimicking me in the blackness of this seemingly dark tomb. It's light above but dark down here. I'm writing all this out because I can see it in my mind that my Dragon has put me out of the way again. If I had stayed on that top deck just a few minutes more I would have been blown over the side like the sailors were. And with all my gear strapped on I would have sunk like a rock!

Just as I grabbed hold of the truck, there was a mighty roar and it felt as though someone behind me had given me a mighty shove forward. Still holding onto the truck, I believe, I was knocked flat and spluttering in the water. As the back end of the barge was lifted in the air there came a deluge of water that knocked the breath out of me. *Jeez! Hell and damnation, we're hit! We're sinking! I've got to get out of here!* I stumbled and fell, and as I write this I see myself completely disoriented, staggering, splashing my way back to where I think the ladder is, water running down from the inside of my helmet, blinding me. As I grab the ladder I'm hoping the truck won't roll back and crush me. I'm pulling at my web belt to get out of some of my gear, thinking I'm going to have to swim. I claw my way back up to the top deck, wildly looking around. *Oh no!* I thought, *not again! I'm fighting the war all by myself again! Where's everybody?! The three sailors are gone!*

I'm soaking and scared. I'm just bobbing in the choppy water while things flash all around me. I'm scared because my mind is going a mile a minute. Even if I could strip naked, my chance of swimming ashore in this maelstrom of bullets, bombs and shrapnel that's churning the water is approximately zero. Anyway, I could never get out of my gear in time, or swim that far to shore. Here I am, I've surely been tagged this time, alone on a sinking barge still a half a mile from shore. *Dad, it don't look good. But I ain't dead yet! Son of a bitch!*

Hanging tight, I'm looking over the side for any sign of the sailors, but see nothing. As I rise up and turn, movement ahead! It's the coxswain popping up from behind the splinter shield! I know I'm in a panic. I'm yelling, but the coxswain, having been down below, knows we're not sinking. "Take it easy," he says, "take it easy, pal. Did you see either of my men?" He's looking too. "Keep a lookout. I'll get you ashore as soon as I get it going again. I want to get you ashore and your load off of here." (Now, I know all these words are not the exact words, but I'm sure close to what transpired). With that the coxswain slid down again into the hole of the engine compartment.

Oh no, no, no, don't do that! Like the guy yesterday who never got back up. Oh, God, have mercy on him. Please bring him back up. I wouldn't go down there for a million dollars. One more near miss and he'll never come up again either!

Frantically I start waving to other barges. But all I get is waves back. No one will stop. Damn sakes! Do they think I'm standing here waving like a Sunday picnicker? Now here's the coxswain again. Thank God he made it back up. Good! Let's get moving the hell out of here. I'm chomping at the bit. I'm less nervous now, that is, until I saw his face. I remember that "I've missed the train" look.

"What! What's wrong?"

He shouted, "I can't, the batteries are fused."

"The batteries are fused? Fused? What the hell does that mean? You mean you can't get started?" I don't know, I just started yelling, cursing and waving again. I hate being scared like this with no chance to shoot back at something. You have to believe firing back can help distract fear. Here I was hoping to get through all this flying shit, and now instead I'm standing still in the middle of it, soaking wet, waving to some idiot sailors waving back. (Oh, hell, I'm off again, in a funk. Excuse me, please.) I just watched as the coxswain made some signals, instead of waving, and got us a tow in the midst of all that flying crap, and I was finally back on the ship amid a lot of yelling and cranes lifting loads over your head. "Stand aside, stand aside!"

Thankfully I watched them lift my bomb into another barge. They waved me down and again I went down the rope net, this time in full daylight. Holy shit! And as soon as I got on board, off we went again. *Oh no! Not another big barge. Is that all they've got?* my mind thought. *Another big target. What am I, a VIP? Again the big whole beloved barge to myself!*

Again I asked, and again it was "Blue Beach!" Oh, Mother! But now at least I can see it's not as bad as it was. The planes and guns seem to be after the "big" guys, the warships, more than the landing barges or the beach. My mind's churning being in another huge barge. Now I'm mad. They never should put one man and a small truck in such a thing, and look what happened to the one I had been in; big as it was, it had a paper ass. Just a near miss. Yeah, it surely was a big near miss, but one near miss and it stops running. Now again, maybe they were afraid I'd blow a hole in the ship; that's why the "here's your hat, there's the door" treatment. Sailors ain't like buddies. I remember I decided no more looking.

I got down with the truck again, those kids above me playing with their 50s. If they can do anything with the planes, it will be to attract their fire. The navy always seems to be filled with fifteen, sixteen-year-old kids the army would never accept. Onboard their favorite pastime is stealing from each other. It's amazing to me as I write this, my mind is saying, "Yeah! Yeah! That's it!" Now mentally I'm back in that big damn barge all by myself. I mean the only soldier on it.

And I have to show all those navy teenagers I'm having just as much fun as them, because it seems that's what they're doing! Whoopee! And I can carry out orders too!

Again I got over to the beloved truck. Everyone should have such a beloved thing. Oh yeah! Sure, I talked to myself, who wouldn't? *Truck*, I thought, *I'm going to get in. Now pull that beloved trick again of never being hit!* I'm all checked out, motor's running, and the fifty's start firing! Those damn navy kids will get us all killed yet! Damn! I keep my eye on the ramp ahead. We must be getting close. At least once I hit the gas I'll be on land and off all these damn boats. I was pressing and caressing the steering wheel and jazzing the motor when I started shaking, and shivering. At first I thought I was cracking up even before I had done anything. But then I realized it was my uniform. It was still soaking wet from the bath I got on the other barge. And besides, I wasn't sick to my stomach. Once I got out of this metal box and into the sunshine I'd be okay. Looking up out of this metal box was like looking up out of my grave. Sitting here shivering was fine; at least my hair wasn't standing on edge.

VIII

THE LONGEST BEACH

Looking at the ramp ahead, I knew when it came down I could expect anything, and I must be ready for it. And then, with a lot of bumping and yelling, it came down. I gave it the gas. I didn't want to stall in the sand. Yet as soon as I cleared the barge I had to stand on the brake. Mines! A long row of them up and down the beach as far as I could see. German Teller mines—at least now we know who we have to fight! All of them are standing on their sides with the detonator looking right at you. Whenever the engineers were in a hurry they would only pull up the first row of mines and stand them on their sides so you could see the detonator and know there was a live field.

I could see a lot of activity over on my right (east). That coxswain *did* drop me off to the west of Blue Beach. He said no to me, but I guess the Germans talked him into changing his mind. Oh yeah! He backed away from me quick enough, leaving my ass almost in the water. Now I'll have to drive east for a ways and stay by the surf to be clear of the mine belt. I'm sure the coxswain saved my butt, and his own, dropping me off here. Most guys don't realize I have a four-wheel bomb. I guess the little truck fools them. But now I have to reach Blue Beach Exit by land, in spite of all those black-cross planes churning up the beach.

I guess I stalled the engine because I jazzed it so much to go and then stood on the brakes so hard because of the mines. Again I went around to the right side so as not to have to climb the spare. As I did I stood back in the sand a little to eyeball the truck. I was about to raise the hood to pull off some of the water proofing around the distributor when suddenly, what's that? I was startled to see this

117

"boat with wheels" come up out of the water on the opposite side of my truck. I was dumbstruck. What in hell? It had a big white star on the side; that calmed me. Actually it was a 6 x 6 truck imbedded in a boat! Like an alligator, I had never heard of one, let alone seen one But it didn't stop; it kept on going up alongside of my bomb and started over the mines. As quick as I thought, *How can it do that?* the front of it with a roar blew up! I went over backwards. Then, without thinking, pure reflex, I dove face down under my truck for shelter as parts and pieces rained down.

I was cursing the other driver for not seeing the mines when he came up on the beach. I was also aware I had, you might say, taken shelter literally in the Dragon's mouth, ergo, the shelter under my truck! The best I can remember, as soon as I could, I got up to run to get away. I had one hand on the truck and one leg headed in the opposite direction. And there's that position again: with eyes wide, mouth open, tongue pressing against lower teeth. Holy Mother, the front end of the "thing" was fully engulfed and blazing to the sky. What about its cargo? If it's shells or any kind of munitions, which it certainly can be, it's good-bye, Mother!

Now, here is a true mental conundrum. Christ, what's a man to think? Run? Run and give it up? No, I can't give up! I know my problem; the engine's flooded. Get in, hold the starter down. Do it! No, don't. Do it! Get outa here! I can't understand or explain. I can't swear the following is actual truth, but to me it is exactly what I did. As I said, with one hand on the "bomb" and one leg wanting to go in the opposite direction, I hesitated, my mind yelling, *Get away! Run!* But at the same time, I'm climbing back in! What am I doing? I'm crazy. Am I being brave? I hadn't thought of that, but I do remember thinking, you're being stupid! Just one piece of that "Thing" blown into the side of mine and everything will be gone, blown away. Wasted! Killing Americans, not Germans. I can't jump! Dragon! Dragon! You bastard, trying to make me run again. I'm going to nurse this baby out of here, because I know I can do it. That's the words. *Do it!*

I can't remember all the rest of the screaming and yelling I did; surely it was the culmination of all the frustrations, sweats and strains I had been through just since getting off the ship. My mind was whirling, sparking; no, that's not the right words. Nevertheless, I'm crying out for help from someone, anyone, to tell me what to do! Reaching, reaching to the innermost depths of my soul, searching. I had the wild feeling of power, something in me coming out, strengthening my mind and body. Is it me? I feel I'm expanding. It's coming out. Think of the Buggers you'll kill with this load! Are you going to die without trying? Think of it! The feeling, bigger and deeper than my father's voice. I'm thinking, *You didn't come this far to run, did you? Like hell I did! Get it out of here! Do it!*

I feel extra strength in my arms and legs. Hey! Hey! The motor's caught on, it's shaking, motor's running. Careful, careful now, move the shift easy, go gentle on the gas, don't spin the wheels. I've got it going! I'm pulling away! I'm pulling into the maelstrom of the beach. Looking back I see the "boat" is still burning, hasn't exploded yet! Who cares? I'm outahere. Holy Hanna!

Looking along the beach, it appears to be like an endless gauntlet. Shit's flying from both sides, under foot and over head. I'm cringing; who wouldn't? Maybe I'm getting back to normal. I'm scared. Damn all the howling and shrieking in the air, just watch for mines. The strength in my arms and eyes getting me along, bucking the endless debris and flying death, trying to head east, where I will find the exit from Blue Beach made by our engineers. I have a purpose, a determination. I'm not writing heroics; I'm writing what's in my mind at the time, cause at the time I was franticly determined to do what I set out to do, with only God or my Dragon sheltering me. Cause this truck is going straight to the captain, going east, or else it's going straight up in the air, departing this earthy vale. Eeeeyow!

Damnation! Remember, I'm not writing about all the things in the war. But there are other men, vehicles and equipment on the beach and in my way. Some things in the way I can't run over, so I keep edging nearer the waterside, where I can get stuck. I must baby my baby. But other than that I pay them no mind. Remember, I'm just putting down my thoughts and feelings and how I managed to cope. The load I carry is important. I have to get it to our base. You gotta know fighting will be severe, and men will need it. So will the captain. I must not lose it, or me.

I came up to a large landing barge on its side, still burning and bobbing up and down with the surf. Oh, terrible! What a sight. Look at the stuff. God almighty. But taking it in with only a scowl, gritting my teeth. I thought, *That's the price we have to pay.* But when I got to the other side of it I saw that it had a large American flag on the stern. The flag was laid out flat in the water, bobbing up and down, with smoke from the flames blowing over it. It looked dead, like the bodies and pieces of bodies bobbing around it. This enraged me. Who wouldn't be? This was not just a "cost of war." This was a desecration! I swore and shook my fist. That flag and those guys ain't dead by a damn sight. The few we are now will soon be an avalanche of thousands and thousands and thousands more of us coming to blow you Buggers away! Oh yes, there I was again, fighting the war alone, howling to heaven, shaking my empty fist at the enemy. But then again, my fist wasn't that empty; it had done a lot getting me this far, getting me to my final destination. I'm fighting alone, desperately alone; that is, with no other men I know. At times overcoming the endless obstacles and obstructions, desperate for another man to boost me on. Like Solan used to do. Just even to say, "That's great, Dave. Don't stop now; we're doing it."

But you know, Dad, my babying this load of death to the Buggers should put my "count" way up there. If I make it. Maybe it won't count as personal, but it will count as something I personally had a hand in! And if I'm killed, or I should say, when I'm killed, my Bugger count should earn me a seat up front. In Scotland's Valhalla. Just as an honorary member, of course. Because I am, and always will be, an American. Proud of my heritage.

Oh shit! Here comes another Buggering black-cross bastard. The AAs blasting and I'm diving again away from the truck. Damn Germans never seem to run out of planes.

Again they're gone. I'm getting up, feeling like I've swallowed some Drano, feeling queer in my gut. It's stupid, but it pleases me to shake my fist at the departing black cross, pursing my lips as I grind my teeth, senseless but satisfying. I'm thinking it's like forever I've been pushing the rig along this stretch of beckoning sandy graveyard. How many more chances am I gonna get?

Getting farther down the beach, I had to stop for some guys in my way. They were setting up some kind of marker for other landings. I did get some curious looks from time to time, as though to say,

What's that guy got under the tarp that's so heavy? But there were still no guys that I knew, and of course, no help. All I could think of to please me was that when I got to the captain I was gonna dig me a big beautiful foxhole, get in and pull a blanket over my head. And bark at the moon. Oh yeah.

Even as I saw the black crosses shooting up the beach ahead, I had new confidence now. I'm getting closer. I'm gonna make it and head inland at that beloved Blue Beach and get to the ammo assembly dump, and may also join the captain to take orders and not have to think for myself. There were other barges and equipment scattered along the beach. I had seen plenty of destruction in Africa, but this was overwhelming. And in such a short time. Worse than the destruction of the nineteen tanks. But I must stick to my goal. Keep going east, threading my way through mainly other guys. No heavy stuff, no tanks or big guns that I remember.

The first destroyed barge I referred to I remembered because it impressed me with its violence. Whatever took it out must have been big, scattering pieces of men and equipment like unholy garbage. From that point on the mess was the same. The endless mess of men and gear seemed to continue, and in my mind, with so much more to come, it would soon make the beach a junk yard. Seeing a half-track burning put my mind back in Fort Knox, again with the instructor talking to us while my eyes were on the brass plate on the dash in front of me. "This vehicle costs $38,000; take care of it." Even now, you might say, with the war just really just getting started, how many of these half-tracks, which were much cheaper I'm sure than Shermans, had I already seen destroyed? The cost must be astronomical. But we were committed and we would continue to bury our enemies in our equipment's might. Till they yelled, "Uncle" Yeah! "Uncle, my uncle."

In those days it took a man's arm to drive a truck or tank. No such thing as "power assist." To shift you had to "double clutch." Remembering the sequence was hard enough, but some tanks had the gear shift just behind your right hip. In others, you sat directly over the drive shaft, cooking your balls. Some guys believed that even if they lived through all this they wouldn't have any functional testicles left to work with when they got home!

Finally I got to where the beloved white tape was farther up from the surf. That's great! Now I have more room to move. Don't have to worry about something jumping out of the ground at me. Now I have only what's flying through the air at me. How many times have I ditched the truck, leaping away, face down? The old feeling of the elephant's legs again. Will the black cross bastard over my head miss me again? Or blow the truck to hell, leaving all my work wasted? And if that's not enough, we have the ship's crew firing at the low-flying strafing planes, adding to the killing of men on the beach by firing their guns too low. And above all this, my wet uniform is plastered with sand! Besides, where in the hell is the exit?

More than once I had to force myself to get back in the truck. With all this shit flying around, I can't see how I'll ever get off this beach. Sooner or later it's got to be me, or the "bomb." No, I ain't quitting. I'll make them make me.

I pass wounded guys motioning at me. What can I do? I have nothing to help them with. And anyway, this damn sure is no sanctuary. The ammo has to get up to the line, wherever that is.

Now I can see a busy spot where vehicles are moving inland. I'm sure I would have had a quicker, easier time of it if I hadn't lost so much time on that stinking, sinking oversized barge. I'll bet the captain must thinking I've been gotten because he's not with me. No, Captain, I don't need no "fairy." I've my own protection, got me a ponderous, putrid "Dragon" wagging his tail over me! He just hasn't decided to dump on me yet. Just a little rich gas every so often so far. To let me know he's there.

Before I got to the wire mesh path over the worst of the sand to go inland, I got up to a row of bodies that had been placed well out of the way. They lie in a row, shoulder to shoulder, waiting, I suppose, to be picked up for burial. Again I thought, that's the cost of war. But one of them hit my heart. Among the bodies was one with the arm and upper part of that side of the body missing—bloody and mangled, but with the face untouched. It was a lieutenant that had given us a "pep talk" back in Algeria. Then, after he was finished, he told us about how his father had a Dodge dealership in Pennsylvania, and after the war he would do good selling cars, because everyone would want one.

Later in the day, we had been called to chow. I saw he had fallen asleep under a tree. I went over, gently squeezing his arm to wake him. "Chow down, sir." I could see he was still in a dream. He said something to me, I wish I could remember, but since I can't, I won't make anything up. After that we had all split and headed for the ships. Now all that was gone, and some dad's dream of a "father and son" would never happen. Worse! Teeth grinding, worse still, no German had done this. The sailor kids on the ships, firing twenty- and forty-millimeter AAs, tracking German planes, inadvertently killed men on the beach. Worse still, some men were so mad they fired their rifles back at the ships! Fortunately, I do believe the ships were out of rifle range. Or so I would hope. I would also hope that the few men killed here by this stupidity would in the future save many lives in the invasions that were bound to come of Europe by limiting the amount of depression on ships' guns in the future.

I would like to pause here for just a moment. That is, as I'm writing this in 2007 I had a meaningful thought about the lieutenant. Somewhere, an older man thousands of miles away in Pennsylvania, a dad, would suffer for the rest of his life knowing he had given up his son for his country, proving a bitter fact: "Freedom isn't free." Another note: I was told later that all of the bodies laid out with the lieutenant had been killed by a 20mm blast from one of the ships. Several others had been wounded. Not by friendly fire, but by stupid fire! And here, as I have explained in my case, the arcane rules of the Purple Heart kick in. They were killed by accident. You know, in the midst of a war, accidents must happen. But sorry, no award! Hope the dad doesn't find out.

Now another note: I have just taken a little hiatus, and now I'm back. It's April 2005. This has been a ball, like trying hard to focus on a crystal ball that works in reverse. I can almost see and feel this young soldier—and he really is a "soldier;" the "line" company saw to that—getting off that huge barge onto a hostile shore on his own. No captain, no buddies, dumped out on the sand, being blown down on the sand, unable to help anyone injured there because of the urgency to move the munitions entrusted to him before they can be destroyed as well. Determined, in spite of the madhouse he's landed in, to get to the fighting men of the First Battalion. His battalion. Damn! Wasn't that a day!? What did I say before? Yeah! THE SOARING HEIGHTS AND FEARFUL, MIND-BLOWING DEPTHS. Oh, man, I really waded in it that day! But I had sworn to myself that no man depending on me would ever have to face the fear, the gutless, helpless fear of being deprived of a weapon in the face of being attacked, as I had been. Ammo must be delivered. And will be if I have to crawl! That's not big talk. That's meaningful talk. On my honor!

Oh well, to get back. I've returned from the VA hospital, this time with pneumonia. The magic plastic bottles that bite into your arms, dispensing more life, so slow, drop by drop, so that it doesn't look too easy. Another hour, another day, another year? Watching the drops, your mind lets go—peaceful, no dreams, no thoughts—only to wake to find you can wisecrack again. Only this time there's a bug. Not only I'm knocking eighty three, but they suspect some trouble with my "counterfeit" stomach, being unable to accept much food at a time. Since I had my quadruple bypass two years ago, I've lost sixty pounds! From 220 to 160. I'm a humble cat now! My rifle has turned into a cane! And I do mean, oh my!

Now to get back, and be advised, this is a continuum, because it is now March 2006 and I'm knocking eighty-four! After a little more work by my hospital, the Salt Lake City V.A—some trouble with my balance and two operations on the eye (info back in chapter one). That eye started to go up in place, causing the eyelid to block the iris. They have had it fixed, so I can still say, I'm still here!

Now to get back to my coming along the beach. There were plenty of other guys around me, but none of my guys. Those beloved Buggers kept shooting up the beach without my ever seeing one of them black cats shot down, but later on I saw more than a few blown into the ground. That was after we got more weapons ashore. Naturally, each time I had to flip off the ignition and take cover under anything except my truck, with my body trying to shrink up into my helmet. I often wondered how much of the beach would be taken out if ever I got tagged, with that many 60mm mortars going off together. Another big danger was the amount of anti-aircraft fallout from all those ships firing up overhead. It had to come down and it damn sure did. As I said before, at times guys would wave to me, but of course they would be waving me away if they knew what I was carrying.

I sorely needed Solan or the captain. I can make it, but I ain't no one-man army. As I pick myself up off the sand time and again, I realize of course all of my yelling and screaming, shaking my fist in the air, is purely a defensive drive to assure myself that I'm not just shoveling shit against the tide. It will in time, in my pursuit, eventually accomplish my goal of causing the Buggers real harm, not just empty threats; it's to relieve my mind. It gives me stamina to go on, even though I can't stand up to the situation with my piece, the piece I once rejected when it was handed to me. To feel its weight as I hefted it, the smell of its breath as I used it, pleasing my eyes beholding the power of its bark as it strikes away the fear in my guts, giving it instead to the Buggers. I carry it in a truck boot. Plenty of room, because there's no cab.

Here on this beloved beach, I never at any time or any other place remember having more weapons thrown against me at the same time, seeing spurts of sand magically jumping all around me. But before I forget, or should I say, while I can, I want to render the fact that come hell itself, I'm so satisfied and happy to have been able, lasting this long, to be what I am—a simple, single GI. A soldier! To have tasted the courage my ancestors' genes, bestowed on me, that gave me strength when I was sorely in need. Also in fighting for my country, I have joined the ranks of the many others who have made us a free people. Sure that's big talk. But if I don't believe I've become a tough-ass American soldier, who will? After all, I'm not that much. But I must keep in mind, I'm something, I am a soldier. And to be a soldier, I have to give it my best. Because, really, that's all it takes. And on top of that, I still ain't dead yet!

Listen up, all you Buggers, I'm gonna succeed. My mind was filled with it; what else could I think? And I'll keep going until either I detonate on this beloved beach, or deliver my goods. If only I had someone to shout in my ear, "Atta baby, Dave, go, go. Don't stop now. You're doing great!" I'm sure, up ahead the captain's watching for me. Blue beach exit! Where the hell is it? That coxswain sure did drop me way short. How about this: Where most guys fight their way ashore and immediately go inland to get off this beloved beach, I have to stay on it, coaxing this load through a maze of scattered destruction, watching for mines beneath and me, those Buggers above me strafing the beach. After heavy stuff, like Tanks.

Still hope the captain made it okay. I know a week or so after I left Solan, I was at Company "A" asking for him. I was told Solan and his new "buddy" had gone out on a patrol one night and never came back. Which meant, of course, if I had still been with him, I wouldn't be here.

Still pushing ahead, I came upon a bunch of guys sheltering under a half-track and laughing. Laughing! What could possibly be funny around here? It was so out of place. I stopped to listen; it was Axis Sally, the sweet propaganda voice for the Germans. She was saying the American First Infantry Division had landed in Sicily by mistake. Can you believe it? They already knew! But the German Army was being kind enough to allow them twenty-four hours to go back to their ships and return to their mothers! For once, I swear I couldn't believe my ears. WHAT! Again I howled with my fist salute. You know me. I bellowed, "You got the right information, lady." Or something like that. "It is the First Division, all of it together. No more fighting by unsupported companies We're going to beat your asses back to Germany starting now!"

Things didn't always go our way. Sure we had some bodies. Ships and barges burning. A ten-thousand-ton ship anchored just off shore that had been burning suddenly blew to bits with a tremendous roar. Fortunately, I'm told, it had been abandoned after fires got out of control. So only its cargo was lost. No lives. All of this was only the down payment of the cost Americans were willing to pay for our freedom. Freedom from any threats to our country. Think of the tremendous cost my generation paid to protect the next generation! In deaths alone, some four hundred thousand! And yet today, when our president warns of our utter destruction, there are those who weep and beat their breasts, crying, "Please bring our boys home," after a cost of some three thousands deaths so far, about the amount we lost in the attack on Pearl Harbor alone. It's hard for people living a comfortable life to really understand that the words "Freedom isn't free" isn't just a slogan; it's a hard, inescapable fact. And until we destroy all of our enemies, whomsoever, and remove any threats to our nation, whatsoever, we will continue to put our youths on the altar to the heart-breaking cost of the parents and loved ones condemned to ever-lasting suffering. I'm sorry I went off again, but it's hard to keep my inner thoughts "inner."

Now to get back. Both the British and the Germans had claimed Americans couldn't fight. Now in the process of their eating their words, I'm sure the British, one of our defamers, were happy they were on our side! In a total of thirty-eight days—that's less than six weeks—we killed, captured or drove off the island of Sicily every German. We took our losses and gave them theirs, while Montgomery was still fighting up the same side of the island he landed on! The few of us who had been rushed overseas and suffered at the hands of the enemies' professional troops were now happy to see our country pouring out the weapons and men in ship after ship full. And especially the new generals, not going by their "promotion" lists anymore, but by experience, General Patton ignoring Montgomery advice. We now had Teddy Roosevelt and Patton, among others, with World War I experience, "fighting generals" that would give us the leadership we needed to make our friends as well as enemies eat their words, eat them down to their socks!

I've said before, many things that happened to me in the army were odd things, like serving my entire hitch as a private, no matter what I was doing. I was a little pugnacious at times, I know, and didn't care for a stripe anyway, or being given one thousand dollars insurance while everyone else had ten. And unlike Senator Kerry, earning three Purple Hearts without spending a day in the hospital, I've spent the last sixty years in and out, being patched up without one. I believe I've mentioned that before. My inquiries to the Army Records Office only bring back a note that they suffered a large fire and my records, among many others, no longer exist. But I'm satisfied. I didn't get the medal, but I did get, and still get, a monetary compensation, which my landlord appreciates better than all my medals. (I did get some, and was awarded three battle stars.) Above all, I lived true to my father's wishes. My manhood suffered some blows, but what can't be held back from me is the fact that in my heart and mind, I still don't lie or steal, and respect women and children. I believe that's manhood, or my best shot at it.

As you may have noted, when all others were laughing at "Axis Sally," I wasn't. I never had any doubts we would beat them. My doubts were when I should start laughing! Those Germans were tough nuts. The ones in Kasserine didn't come at us in tanks; they were on foot, running and climbing over broken rock, yelling! I wonder if our guys could do that? Maybe the schnapps helped.

Speaking of tanks, I haven't seen any, ours or theirs. But I see LSTs out there; they must be bringing ours in. They better do it quick; I'm sure the Germans pelting us with their aircraft continuously are aware of our lack of tanks.

Engineers have put down some matting so that we can get over a patch of soft sand. Beyond, on harder ground, I see one of those "ducks" tried to climb the side of a mound and now has ten wheels in the air, completely turned over, with half a guy—his legs and hips—sticking out from under. No attempt to dig him out? He surely must be squashed, and probably no pulse.

Now, there's some nice beach houses. Oh yeah! With walls two-feet thick of concrete—pill boxes made to look like cottages. Maybe the first wave didn't have it so easy. I just passed what I guess was their first line of defense, including the disguised pill boxes. The "ducks" and trucks were unloading supplies, and this area was my goal, where I was to meet Capt. Kendal. I wasn't looking around at the Jeeps. I knew the captain wouldn't have wheels till I delivered his "bomb" and accompanying load to him. Okay? Oh yeah!

IX

BACK WITH THE CAPTAIN

Hey! Hey! There was the captain. I made it; how about that? I stood up holding the steering wheel and gave a wave. In his bland, usual, nonplused way, he waved back. That's great! If ever you could find someone to stand by that gave you confidence and fortitude, there he was. A great relief flushed through me. Now I didn't have to make all the decisions myself anymore, as I had been on my seemingly endless quest from the shores of Algeria through the endless assaults of man and nature. Hey, that's quite a line. A "quest." I looked it up in my book of words (dictionary) to be sure I had the right meaning. As follows: quest—heroic expedition in search of a particular object. Right on! And there he was. And of course this particular "end" meant only a big new beginning. Now we would have to work harder than we did in Africa.

He needed a reconnaissance up above us to see what lie ahead. We didn't go far. The truck was still loaded. We went north to a long row of dunes running parallel to the beach. From there it was slightly downhill to a black macadam road running along the beach. Beyond the dunes a huge anti-tank ditch ran north and south out of sight. The ditch came all the way down from the far hills and ended on the north side of the road. That didn't seem to make much sense, for with the road there anyone could easily cross over the ditch. Not crossing over to the north side of the road, we dismounted and climbed some small dunes and could see the extent of the huge plain. Suddenly there was a lot of firing behind us—a German plane no more than twenty feet above the dunes behind us, flying flat and straight, not firing, and really not a threat to us. It was off a way, but by no means a long way. I went down on a knee when I saw it, ready for anything. But then it was obvious the pilot was either dead or unconscious. It continued on despite all the fire it drew till reaching the far hills; it simply crashed into them, exploding. And someone was heard to say: "Well, there's one good German."

After getting a fair look around, we went back to the beach, back to our temporary dump. My memory is vague here. We stashed the load up there in some kind of depression. I think it's vague because what's coming up is overwhelming. The worse situation the Dragon ever cooked up, then laughingly switched the tail to get me out almost too late.

Later, things were quiet; no black crosses overhead for a while. Where I had parked the truck was like on tough turf around and between the sand dunes. I could see the LSTs (landing ship tanks) were beginning to unload. I was sitting on the turf and had just lain back, my arms comfy behind my head to take, as they say, "ten." My eyes were resting on the empty sky overhead. It's nice to get some rest in the daytime, especially when I'm being paid almost as much in the army as I got bustin' my ass in the shipyard. Way, way up I spotted a tiny dot coming along the sky all by itself. All hands on the beach were busy, no guns hammering, which was a pleasant, quiet moment. My eyes had fastened on the dot. Now, I wouldn't doubt I was the only guy to see what happened from start to finish. As the dot that had attracted my attention came closer, it started a gradual descent. Now it's dropping straight down over by the LSTs. It is! It's a dive bomber! Jeez, doesn't anyone see it? Are all the ship gunners asleep? There, it's arcing away.

I sat bolt upright. I could see a smaller dot continuing on down. Holy hell! The anti-aircraft blasts at everything a mile away; here's one right over their heads and not a shot! Now they start shooting. But it's to late. I watched the smaller dot, such a tiny thing, not knowing until later that I was seeing the death of forty men. That was the count. Our complete "Cannon Company," guns, trucks, tanks, artillery, rations, with all the ammunition plus an entire ship, by, I assume, one man, in one plane, with one bomb. He hit dead center on LST #313. I never forgot that number. Though I'm not superstitious, I always pass that number by. His act certainly raised our cost of war.

You think I remember a lot? How could I ever forget that! When

I watched the bomb hit, I thought, *Great! It landed between two LSTs and the brown plume was sand and dirt.* Unfortunately I was wrong; that bastard was right on! Dead center.

He had come over by himself—there were no others—and only drew fire as he left. I'm sure he was another brave enemy and must have earned a bag full of Iron Crosses. But now, without our "Cannon Company," we were going to be in a bad way when that inevitable German counter-attack hit.

Coming down from the hills I thought we would be back to fighting like a scrub team again! But no, I said it and it was true. It was no longer "some" of us were here, from here on out "all" of us were here! And that included the U.S. Navy. We didn't get our cannon company ashore, but we did get some ensigns with their radios to direct the fire from our warships on the enemy. And I was to see in the future both German tanks and infantry flee in front of it. Hot damn! Stand up and cheer! Run, you bastards, run!

Another time my fearful eye was on an approaching tank when one of those unbelievable howling shrieks from a ship hit it. It didn't knock it out, it dissipated it. You know, dissipate: to scatter, to disperse, to drive completely away, make disappear! Only a big hole in the ground, pieces falling through the air. Germans, you've kicked a tiger in the ass and now it's going to bite off your balls. You'll see how we fight, and it may cost some, but we'll make you wish you were fighting Frenchmen.

One thing France can take credit for—their act of surrendering so early and so easy gave Hitler what the Japanese called "victory disease," and he went into Russia with his newly reconstituted army and air force before they were fully ready, and of course no intelligence of the hidden monster he was attacking, thinking he had another France to take out. With soldiers of poor fighting qualities (sound familiar?), sure he trounced them, because they weren't ready, at first. But instead of surrender, those brothers got together, and until this very day no one can say for sure how many millions of men, tens of thousands of tanks and planes he caused to have thrown at him.

Now, unbelievably, as if he didn't have enough enemies destroying his "Superman" army, his "flashing sword," he declared war on the United States along with the Japanese. And to comply with their wishes for war, this pisspot of a nation, Japan (if you can believe, actually smaller than California alone, not to mention our other forty seven states), you could say was like a very strong man, and they were in their capacity very strong, but this very strong man decided to attack a gorilla, causing the United States to produced the following (statistically correct): over 30,000 heavy bombers, more than 40,000 fighter planes, ten new battleships, several hundred destroyers, nearly 3,000 merchant ships, nineteen fleet (that's large) carriers, and more than eighty, yes eighty, small carriers. The "Greatest Generation" had a lot of help.

Fortunately all this was done prior to the birth of the news media. The people at home were fed results, not bathos. But with the advent of the television of today, now they feed us what they believe, to show how smart they "iz." If my generation had the blinding, distorting news and a daily body count, not of the enemy, but of our guys, and if they had been in power then, we might have quit after initial disasters, went home to Mother, and we would all be speaking German in one half of the country and Japanese in the other half. Oh yeah! Like hell!

You know, I make disparaging remarks about the French, but the toughest fighting men in the world can count for nothing when led by cowardly and gutless leaders. Like someone once said, I would not fear an army of lions led by a sheep, but an army of sheep led by a lion is a different matter. And here we were, an army of lions led by a lion. Time for someone to start fearing.

The surrender of the French to save themselves, only to become literal slaves to a country that had been in manpower and weapons *smaller* than themselves, must be pacifism to the extreme. To comply with any and all demands of their occupiers, supplying the war material to be used on their neighbors, serving to cut the will of smaller nations, leaving their best ally, England, overwhelmed without a chance to fight, this should go into our history books with a roar; instead there's hardly a whimper. Why? It would be a very different world today if our country hadn't stepped in to fight for everyone. Including the thankless French.

Sorry I've run off again. Now back to the beach. Our beach was a mess; no one could get near the burning, exploding 313. Some were trying to pull men out of the water who had jumped or been blown from the ship. One LST next to it was backing away with its doors open. The other just sat there, I guess unable to move. I hope it doesn't go up too! To think, the German came down in the center of all those guns and never drew a shot! Wonder what kind of fairy he's got?

Now the captain is back. He said we didn't have to load up, but we had to go up again for another look around, this time with a major in tow. He was to check out our advance right away. Looking at this guy, the major, and listening to him reminded me of the other smart-ass officer, the captain, back in Africa, who wouldn't believe me about the misfiring of the B.A.R. I often wondered if part of his head went with the shots through the shingles! The major's attitude was on the same level. Another man who had reached his level of incompetence. "Boy, you can't tell me anything; you don't know how smart I 'iz.'" Oh, Mother, here we go again!

Now, with the major we were to go back up to where we were looking around earlier, only this time we continued across the macadam road driving north out into the open field, alongside the big anti-tank ditch on what had been the enemy's side (less chance of mines). As we went up alongside the tank ditch, we saw on our side a crane of ours unloading some truck—I mean some "duck" truck— cargo out in the field. I couldn't help wondering how in the hell anyone managed to get a crane ashore before unloading our tanks or other heavy weapons that were sure to be needed for defense. Our cannon company should have been ashore by now, but of course they were history in the wreckage of LST 313, giving a perfect example of why more guns and weapons should have been unloaded first. The enemy is known for always counter-attacking as soon as possible. Again, examples of incompetent officers.

Again I sound as though I'm picking on officers. But I do include a specification—incompetent; it's the incompetent ones, high or low, that cause the greatest harm and undo the efforts of the competent ones. I have apparently by observation in my short time in the army acquired the ability to spot "balognas in bars" who rely more on bullshit than brilliance. I mean, look, how are you going to stop a counter attack with a crane? Well, to get on, I must repeat, it's not that I'm so smart, it's just the way things work out sometimes.

The major and the captain were talking as the major continued to motion me ahead with his hand. I felt a little raised in my seat, or should I be more specific and say nervous. Prescience? I don't know. We had just left an area with hundreds of guys, but now we were going out into a vast, empty, open field where I saw nobody. I could now understand how all those guys with Columbus felt sailing into a void.

I heard the major exclaim, "Well, it's about time we got some tanks up here."

What? Great. I turned around to look. Nothing! There's nothing back there. What does he mean? He's looking ahead. He's right. Tanks! Tanks? There up ahead of us, tanks. I hit the brake. They can't be ours, unless they unloaded some time ago farther up the beach. And if they had gotten that far in already, they wouldn't be coming back. All this flipped through my brain in an instant.

"What's up, soldier?"

"They do look like tanks, sir, coming at us head-on. It's hard to tell, but they can't be ours." (I'm putting in words I can't swear to, but they average out.)

"Nonsense, soldier! Why can't they be ours? Even if they're not, they may be British. We were told they would be landing somewhere up on our right."

Now, I'm not talking to just another guy. He's a major. Maybe he knows something more than I do about where the British landed. But then one of them started to move to the flank. The *right* flank! He's coming from the left! Oh, Christ! That low silhouette, that's no American! Or British! My heart dropped. I flipped the ignition off. Bail out! They're German!

They jumped, and me after them. In the tank ditch the major wanted to know what made me so sure they were German. I opened my mouth, but I didn't have to answer. Ripp, Boom, Bam, Ripp, Boom, Bam. Oh no, I thought, not that again. Christ, how do you fight a gun a mile away?

I had fallen next to the truck, holding onto it. I climbed out of the ditch to get my weapon in the boot, and also so as not to show the officers that I was going to throw up. I was holding onto the truck because that damn sickness had hit me again! I wanted to throw up.

I couldn't let them see me do that. I had to get my piece out of the truck; there'll be infantry with them. Another shot ripped by me. Holy hell! The next one will get the truck! Even if it's empty, I don't want to go up with it. I turned around and ran.

We've got to get out of here, back to the sand dunes by the macadam for cover. If I try to move the truck they'll pick us off. The captain and major didn't need any more urging; they had already taken off. I scrambled along the steep side of the ditch, but I could make no headway there—the sand was too loose. I got to the top and started to run. I could see the crane was down. I'll bet they thought it was some kind of gun. The tanks were coming faster now. I struggled to catch up to the officers. Oh, man, what am I going to do? What can stop them? Our cannon company is on the wreck of the ship. I haven't seen any of our tanks yet. Whip cracks over head, bullets! Gotta get down.

Suddenly up ahead, I mean back at the dunes and the macadam road, a lot of firing breaks out. Germans must be flanking us. And just for the moment I feel licked. I'm not throwing up, but I've got the heaves. I'm gonna be caught again without a weapon! I had determined with all my might after Kasserine that I would never ever be without a weapon again! But now again the Dragon has dealt me from the bottom of the deck.

My eye was now on the proximity of the tanks. There were more of them now! And much closer, gaining on me. How the hell did I ever get in a spot like this? I've got to get going. Looking back at them advancing, firing at us, coming at us. We have some shells falling among them Buggers. Good! That means we have some guns going. But right now my only hope is to get back to the dunes.

I'm panting; it doesn't look good. If I gotta be killed, it's got to be running, not laying down! Here I am again, Super Son of a Bitch, without a weapon, running for my life with no possible chance to hit back! Dragon! Dragon! You've failed me. They're going to chop up my ass with their tracks. Even if they don't run me over, their infantry will get me. What are you doing? I mean, they're close now! Dragon! Dragon! Then, crrraaaack! Rooomboom! Love a God! Right over my head, again and again, concussions battering the helmet on my head, like a Dragon's big feet kicking dirt and sand into my prone head and hands hugging the ground. Jeez! It must be them. We don't have anything like that! Give me strength! Again! Wow! Hey! Whooosh, Boom! I feel the pressure. Now I'm down on my face. I'm not grasping it this time, I'm pounding it. Damn, damn, damn.

I begin to lift myself up on one arm, squinting back just past my elbow to see what's firing at me just in time to see one of the tanks coming at me turn into a black scattered explosion with the next tremendous slam, blown to bits, fortunately pieces blowing away from me. Head back in the sand I'm thinking, *It can't be! Is it real?* Of course, although it was just a mad coincidence, my mind accepted it as an answer to my Dragon's plea. I forgot! There's a navy out there! It's got to be the navy.

A battleship, what else? The ones I saw around us on that second trip I took on the oversized ship's barge before they finally got me ashore. You can't blame me for forgetting; we never had the navy back us up before. But now look what they have done. I sure hope that hill or dune back there they're firing over won't let them fire any lower, or they'll turn me into an "unknown but to God." Cock a doodle! I could crow!

Now I can hardly see, half blinded by the dirt and sand blown in the air and over me. But I'm dancin', yeaah bo. Born again! Howling and dancing, man! Damn! You Germans are not attacking some unsupported rifle companies anymore or some guy like me without a weapon. Them's my boys out there, sailors in a mighty ship, American sailors. Now us guys, just riflemen, can call on Zeus with his many and varied lightening bolts, from the ground, the sky, and even from the sea, to blow your asses, tanks, and even the 88s away. Sure! I'm riding up on the Dragon's back again, ecstatic because only a little bit ago I was crawling under his belly, puking, knowing this time I'd surely be finished, and again without a weapon. Imagine! We can call on a battleship.

I'll never know who that ensign was. It's gotta be one of them ensigns with his transmitter; all I'll ever know was that he was a brother, a fellow American, whose exact coordinates sure did save me. With him and his little transmitter (and that big beautiful battleship) and its triple pounding shots one after the other, we're going to go through the enemy like crap through a goose!

Now just a note: Remember, I'm writing about my most inner thoughts as I dance with the Dragon, thoughts I would never divulge before. But since I'm soon to be a memory, you can have them. Because that's the way it was.

It wasn't until 1977, thirty-three years later, when I met a navy veteran at the VA. Reminiscing, I told him about what I owed the navy, about the battleship at first scaring me so, firing right over my head, destroying and chasing off the German tanks, leaving me dancing in the sand, crowing like a rooster, feeling as though I had done it all by myself. Nodding his head he laughingly said, "That's great! But that was no battleship. That was my ship, a cruiser."

His job was in the engine room, below deck. They were always kept informed over the speakers when the ship was firing what the target was and the results. And they were told they had stopped an attack on Gela Beach and were chasing the Germans back. Now again, no fiction, matter of record. The name of his ship was the *U.S.S. Brooklyn*. How about that! We had run away from my little truck with its Brooklyn flag on the hood. But the Germans never got to it because a bigger, much bigger "Brooklyn" came along. Oh yeah!

Now for sure you must think I'm laying it on you with the story of the *U.S.S. Brooklyn,* the cruiser I thought was a battleship. But even trying not to make a big thing of it, it was a big thing to me. Now I had that feeling that I'm ten feet tall and my name's Godzilla. Imagine the headlines in the hometown newspaper, the *Brooklyn Eagle* (a real newspaper): DAVID LAWRIE'S BUTT SAVED BY U.S. NAVY! Battleship makes enemy scatter before becoming scatter themselves. Think of it, my country providing me with a battleship when I needed a weapon. How can we lose? I'm elated, who wouldn't be? Sure I danced, whooped and howled like an Indian dancing in the sand. I had to swallow too many downers, I mean like way down, rotten downers, overwhelmed and forced to run for my life too many times, and this was an upper I would never forget, and I wanted to enjoy it to my wildest! Hell, we're on an island. The navy can follow us all around it!

Now, I still haven't made anything up. Reading back over what I have written, I see my writing goes from a high point to a low point, then again a high point, zoom down to the low. It was easy writing like that because that's the way it was. It seems my Dragon has flicked his tail again to keep me around, for what reason I'll never know. He seems to be on my side, but has a hell of a way of showing it. I'm sure he's the reason, when I finally got home, I had a strip of gray, no white hair my wife aptly called my "German hair" along the side of my head. And, you know, I think she had it right.

It was unfortunate for us who were the first over against the tough and disciplined soldiers the Germans were, plus their proven weapons of four years experience against our "pre-owned" World War I equipment. Plus the fact they owned the sky, since we had no amount of planes to speak of to retaliate. And pity the poor bastards who manned our newest tanks, being blown away by huge tanks and guns we had nothing to compare with. But in coming down so hard on us in the beginning, they "learned" us. Yes, I know my English. But I still say they learned us, the hard way, and we kept on learning. Sure we eventually had overwhelming industrial strength. But it was "method" we lacked. And our learning to fight their way, plus our material strength, led to their ultimate defeat and eradication. But that was still a long bloody trail to go.

I knew in my heart that we would in time get together a "real" army and become, as post-war authors have written, a "Band of Brothers." Think of it, just as I have described my helplessness, unarmed, out of position in the face of an advancing enemy, others on board a ship, Americans, my "brothers," not only saved my butt, but gave the enemy a bloody nose! Who can stop us?

Sure, that's great, but now my mythical, maniacal Dragon was about to show me through its teeth what we still lacked. Leadership! In our upper echelons of experienced fighting generals. What we needed was the type of hard know-how generals like the Germans had, not the inept guesswork of general (desk) officers, with their decisions approved by Eisenhower, like their decision to fly in paratroopers over the heads of our ships and even over the First Infantry Division fighting on the ground. Unbelievable! And that ended up a disaster!

That evening, directly on the heels of a stream of German bombers that had been working us over all day, constantly over the ships and beach, American paratroop planes, just at dusk, followed along like sheep on their compass course. Then I would say out of some thousand ships in our invasion fleet, some hundred, at least, were off our beach. And all were blasting away at planes both German and American. Every man ashore had to take cover from the zip, whip, whip, whack, smack of the almost vertical AA falling from the sky. Suddenly I heard yelling above the constant firing. "Paratroops! Paratroops!" Oh, yeah! I've heard that enough times before. Nervous guys. But look, its true! To hell with cover, get those bastards! Get them before they hit the ground. Fire! Fire! Pull the trigger. Pull the trigger, and move. Always move after you fire, if you can, before someone spots your position. They couldn't get to the beach with their tanks, now they're trying it with paratroops. Fire! Fire!

I can only fire up. To fire lower, I might hit our own guys on the ground up ahead. Then with the last few shots going off, it's suddenly over. There's yelling and screaming, but no more shooting and the AA has stopped. I've got my back up against some gear piled up next to me, hoping to cover my back. I'm trying to keep my panting down. I'm alert, highly alert. Shoot and you might draw attention. Shoot and it might be one of our guys. Although, if he has any brains, he'll hold still like me. The shadows, just like standing guard; did it move? Was it there before? Keep your eye on it. Watch it. Watch it. I'm exhausted. I'm making no attempt to stay awake. It's been a hell of a day. Christ! I always seem to be fighting the war alone.

The next thing I remember, the captain's voice is rousing me. It's daylight now. "Dave, Dave, it's okay, it's over. It was all a mistake." I can't remember the exact words of the captain. He was saying we had to get going; we had some wounded, but none of our guys had been killed, only the paratroopers, unfortunately American paratroopers.

"What! What! Who told you that!? What did you say?"

"Easy, Dave. Remember, we could only see their shapes and shadows."

Yeah, I remember, just seeing them come down. But naah, they would never jump on top of us. That don't make no sense.

I got up, head buzzing, wondering what kind of Alice in Wonderland I was in now. The captain said, "Come on, Dave. Get your gear back in the truck; we've got to get going."

If there was wounded, they were already gone. But the dead, and there was enough, had been pulled to the side of the road, like the ones down on the beach. You could tell small arms killed them; they weren't badly torn up. I didn't want to write this, but it's part of my promised sojourn, something I tried for years to forget. Oh yeah!

Now the pencil has turned up a very bitter memory. I had to get out of the truck and look. I had to see these guys for myself. The guys were all wearing brown. All of us, that is the First Division men, hit the beach wearing green fatigues. No one had ever seen cups on helmet straps, and weapons that could fold up, and boots, not leggins! Germans never wore leggins; they wore boots. What the hell other confusion was there? And if I was young, all of these guys seemed younger, with not one hairy, ugly German in the bunch. I went back to the truck, my insides raging. How could they possibly make such mistakes?! Again! What's next, for Christ's sake?!

For the second time I felt I had enough. Let me go home. Disgusted and trembling, I put the truck in gear and moved out. Down the road, not even a mile, there's a group of guys trying to sort out this pile of arms, heads, boots and ammo webbing.Glider men. Again, I felt, Jeez! For Christ sake! Our guys shot down on the beach by our ships, then paratroops blown out of the sky and shot up by us; now here's a glider, a bunch of guys stuffed in a box made of cardboard and balsam wood with the weight, whatever guns, Jeeps, ammo, in the back to balance it. But the weight, when it crashes, it acts like a meat grinder, crushing everyone to dog meat! And all of this done without one German raising a finger! And worse still, you can't get rid of the people responsible for this.

I'm sorry. I've gone off again. But I'll bet if the people designing those gliders had to ride in them, they would come up with something designed to destroy the equipment in a crash. Not the men. Hopefully these hard lessons will lead to better procedures to saving ourselves from ourselves in future invasions. And there will be! We won't stop! The "Dragon" surely got a full meal today. Oh yeah!

After that the Germans were falling back, and in time we were moving ammo dumps and the field train forward, past heaps of smashed German wagons, dead horses and men scattered along the road, compliments of the fly boys and the artillery. Now I got to see those black crosses smashed, burning to the ground, making our life on the roads a lot easier. Everywhere we saw remnants of the great German Army. Gritting my teeth and pinching my eyes looking, I knew it! I knew if I lasted long enough I'd see my countrymen, my brothers here and at home, together forming an army bigger than Portugal's and having the most men who "can't fight" tear these bastards to pieces. Everywhere I went I saw evidence of the planes, the big guns and our guys with the rifles. Men, emigrants, from every country in the world becoming naturalized Americans, fighting alongside of the rest of us in our uniform, putting it to the supermen. Sure they jumped us in Africa with their know-how and better equipment, but now it was going to be their turn to holler "unfair."

Sorry, but I have to put down my feelings. And my feelings were always the same: Give it to them, grind them into the ground!

Now to let up a little. One particular day we had halted in an area covered with motorcycles. Seems some Italian motorcycle regiment not wanting to fight Americans had simply taken off, leaving their bikes behind. The bikes weren't heavy like U.S. bikes, but much lighter and easier to handle. Now, in Fort Knox they had a motorcycle school, and men so assigned were taught there. This one day that we mixed in with them, one of their guys had shown me how easy they were to operate, with the controls being on the handles. And, of course, with only the open air and your shirt for protection, I decided he was nuts, and I would rather have the protection of a tank!

I remembered how heavy the U.S. machine was, and how awkward it was spreading your legs to get on. But it really was more fun than work. Now, here in Sicily the bikes were light and little more than motorized bicycles, so picking one up alongside on the road, I jumped on to try it, and, Whoopee! Quickly familiarizing with it, I drove it up and down the road. Then, unfortunately, to show the captain how fast I could go, I gave it the gas, and *zoom*, off I went. But not far, because my helmet blew off and, without thinking, I grabbed for it with both hands. Letting go of the handles was a mistake! The front wheel tucked in, and over I went, flying up the road on my bare right arm. Ouch! Ouch! Ouch!

Dripping blood and dirt, I had lost a patch of skin from my wrist to my elbow. Now I could understand why Indians, sorry, I mean Native Americans would skin people before burning them. Being skinless hurt like hell, like liquid fire, even after cleaning and having a soothing balm applied by a laughing medic. And again, surmise, war is hell. Also, be happy the U.S. Army has replaced bikes with Jeeps.

Now, you know, a lot of times going back and forth from our dump to the line companies I was alone. My only distractions were what I was looking at, leaving possibly too much time to think. Getting past the men lining the road, tired men, guys I could see more than a few times looking at me and the little tarp-covered truck as though to say, "Whose the private driving alone?" Of course, they wouldn't if I offered them a ride and they found out I was even carrying sympathetic bandolier torpedoes on top of how many clusters of mortars? Oh! Let 'em eat their hearts out. I served my time in the line. Now I may ride to hell, but at least I'll be riding. And making note of how many of those big, dead German tanks our fly boys took out sure picks up my spirits. Oh yeah!

There's no doubt, our air cover and the mighty ships and guns of the navy firing far into the island gave us the support we needed. And gave the Germans a taste of what we faced at first in Africa.

Now, I didn't have far to go from the ammo dumps to the line. One time I had to stop to help two guys with a Jeep and a trailer blocking the road. I had to help them lift a dirty, bloody body bag into the Jeep trailer. It was like lifting a big bag of jelly. A driver of a 6 x 6 had passed an obstruction that had been placed in the road as a warning to tell a bridge was out. All of the bridges along this cliffside road were made of two or three arches. The Germans would inevitably blow out the road between the arches. The truck landed on its nose at the base of what was left of the opposite arch, crushing the driver between the engine and the load on the truck. I didn't ask if they got him out in one piece. I just wanted to help get them out of my way. Death has endless ways to tap your shoulder.

Other things can happen to the young, inexperienced soldiers that we were besides being killed. When we first started moving inland we found fields and fields of melons, and I, along with others, waded into a melon feast, anything being better than the same old rations. It was great until I got stricken with the "Axis of Evil" revenge. And the grand insult to my bowels didn't stop there. Just as it was foretold, when I went to squat flies took position on my butt, then with infinite patience waited and rode it down. What a country! The only thing that made it bearable, even laughable, was the thought of the Germans going through the same thing. Only their army didn't supply toilet paper! It's true; we actually got some toilet paper in some of our rations. How about that! The problem was getting any goodies past the rear guys.

The following is a kind of involved story, but I'm reminded of it to tell of how different men behave when facing death, and how precious life is to all.

I had parked just off the road (dirt, as usual) on, I should say, the "up" leg of a Y just a little ways from an ambulance. It was safe, Germans long gone, didn't need to dig a foxhole. The ambulance crew had picked this spot, same as me, to shack up for the night. That evening we had come to a, I guess you would call it, a reverse Y. I could manage to go from the downside of the Y to the upside by making a loop, but a bigger vehicle couldn't do that. It would have to swing around as far as it could go, then by backing and filling come forward again to gain the other leg. I had gotten around by pulling close to the edge of the road, then making a continuous 180-degree turn to the left. That put my right front wheel to the edge of the road again to put me on the upside. These explanations are necessary. And you can use a pencil if you want.

So you can imagine where the German patrol that had gotten that far back placed their mines, right? One on each side of the Y, where a vehicle backing and filling to make the turn would inevitably drop a wheel off the road. We hadn't been the only ones to make it safely. An ambulance, and several Jeeps with officers had also gone up this leg. Although I thought later I was lucky the Dodge could make it without dropping a wheel, it wouldn't have got me. It was on the captain's side. But since it might have killed him, his fairy kept my wheels on the road. Oh yeah!

The captain had bedded down in the officers C.P. and I was asleep on the truck's camouflage net and my blanket when there was a terrific explosion. I was instantly face down, guts churning. And then, of all times to do it, I couldn't find my forty-five and flash light that I always slept with. I hugged the ground, flat and terrified. What's coming? Brain racing, I started crawling away from the truck, thinking it didn't sound like a mortar. Hell, I didn't hear a plane, and nothing incoming.

Finding my piece and flashlight, I got a sudden thought. The sound was the same as when the truck with the duffel bags blew out its rear wheel. It was a mine. The flat double *Bam!* was the same. Then a lot of yelling and screaming down by the Y. And then a loud voice bellowing, "Don't let me die! Don't let me die!" Men on their knees down by the Y holding flashlights on something or someone in front of a wrecked truck, a 6 x 6. Please, I'm not adding anything to this. This was nerve-wracking enough without any ugly descriptions. I added my light to the others in the front. There was a medic, no helmet, just an arm band, working to tie off the guy's stump. The leg looked exactly like a ham steak, with the round bone in the middle. And you can believe every time I have ever sat down to ham steak and eggs, I can hear that loud, raucous, bellowing voice, "Don't let me die!" I had to keep holding my light on this to enable others to work, and all the while the guy kept bellowing, "Don't let me die!" Others were working on the other leg, mangled and shredded to the bone.

Now, perverse as this may seem, both men were very lucky. The medics sleeping in the ambulance were instantly on the scene, clamping off the man's arteries. Both legs were lost, but the captain told me later he made it and was on his way back to the States. The driver, we were told, had just turned his head to look out the side. He got cut up, but didn't loose his eyes. Remember, everything is relative. In relation to blind and dead, both men were lucky. And so were we all when the engineers dug up the mine on the other side that we didn't know was there! Oh yes! Oh yes!

My reverse crystal ball works with things that made an impression on me. Unfortunately the banal talk and the everyday routine escapes me. That is, after sixty years, who's wouldn't? Even trying to get the things that impressed me in proper sequence at times gets mixed up, although most of the time I'm pretty close.

I do believe we were headed back to the beach for some reason, and I was stopped by MPs. What I noticed that was unusual was the fact that all the MPs were packing Thomsons. A Thomson is a short submachine gun. An MP usually carried a rifle and looked like an ordinary soldier wearing an armband and markings on his helmet.

X

The MPs, and there were many, were waving their arms in a chopping motion, seeming to say: sit still and shut up! The captain got out to see what was up. One of the cradled Thomsons waved him back, shouting, "Patton! Get back." And, oh boy, here comes the parade. Big Daddy, the chief, our "leader," General Patton himself. He was standing up in his vehicle, and so was I to get a better look. I wasn't waving, just standing, maybe a little dirty, soiled, but looking very attentive. I can't swear, but as he passed I believe for a couple seconds we made eye contact. His eyes were hard, no wimp there. Then I would like to believe I got an approving, curt nod! Man, it was great! Imagine, those piercing eyes had given me a nod! I felt great, like ten feet tall. I don't know what I looked like, but I was sure I got his nod. And I was the proudest private in the army. Imagination or not, he sure made me feel that I really counted. I can't say whether I impressed him or not, but he surely impressed me! He really did have a fierce look, or was he squinting in the sun? And he really did wear cowboy six-shooters. I wonder if they were loaded? But you could damn sure bet those Thomsons were. What a parade! But if he was as good as they say, let him primp and posture around all he wants. Besides being 100 percent American, his ancestors, all from Scotland, had fought in every American war. And my being an American soldier of the same Scotch descent, it suited me fine.

Nothing can beat the feeling of pride. "Hey, Captain, look at my chest!" Expanded by a nod. General Patton just gave me a slight payment for all the shit, debris and murderous fear I've waded through to get here, and given me the will to keep going, although I do believe I have developed an antagonistic view of the Buggers after me. (I

145

like that word, "antagonistic." It's a fancy, educated way to spell, h.a.t.e. Oh yeah!)

Some time later, after the last German had been driven from Sicily, the limeys were beginning to believe we could fight. From here on out any snide remarks on their part would be hollow ones, because the only reason the British finally got up the east side of the island was because we cleared the Germans off the top, and the Germans made a final leap to the Italian mainland to get away. Anyone, especially Japanese, saying we wouldn't or couldn't fight, and the German Bitch with her "Go home to Mother" crack, bastards all, not giving us a chance to get it together; now we could say to all, "You ain't seen nothin yet."

Now to get back to Patton. After the island was cleared and we had been pulled back to Licata and Gela, where we had invaded, Patton gathered together the entire First Infantry Division in a field and stood on a newly built wooden podium to tell us all, in his inimitable style, to put down any rumors of going home. We were all amazed at his voice. I'm sorry to say it was more squeaky than even light thunderous. I guess one of God's little jokes. "Listen up, you men have done nothing yet! Now we're going after the Hun where he lives!" What else he said was lost in the murmur of discontent. Oh well.

"Going after the Hun were he lives" in my mind meant no stopping until Germany and Japan were nothing but piles of rubble, or some other kind of offal, the offal I would say that they themselves planted. I believe he also added, "Since the German Army has taught the First Division how to fight *their* way, the First Division will have the honor to lead the way. The Germans have earned destruction, and we will pay them off."

Despite many unhappy guys, we all gave him a mighty yell. "Go, Patton, go!"

Yeah, good old "Blood and Guts" Patton. And as everyone knew, it was our blood and his guts. Just show us the way!

Maybe a crystal ball really is mystical, but I feel in all honesty that to read or write about, or to have actually been a participant in this violence, no one can be squeamish about what they write if they're to write in truth.

Well, anyway, as great as I thought his speech had been, many others viewed it like, "Hey, we fought this far; let someone else try it for awhile."

I was disappointed. It wasn't much of a pep talk, and what came next was even worse! Stunning! He was apologizing. Apologizing? At first no one knew if it was some kind of a gag, or what? No, he really was saying he was sorry that instead of punching a guy, he had actually slapped him in a fit of gloved fag rage! Oh, man! All that tough talk, hand guns and fierce looks, and he slapped someone! I'm sure that's not the way Rommel would have done it to one of his guys. What a downer. We found out later, though, that he had to. It was the beginning of the news media, the power of the press, vilifying anyone or anything for the greater glory of the new leaders of America, the American press! Picky, picky. Pick a good one and pick up your bonus. For a big hit. Lousy snakes in the grass. All for money, and their thoughts of how smart they "iz," to keep us peasants informed properly.

Oh well, How about a laugh? I give you my "pancake day":

Did I ever tell you about the "armor" they issued us in World War II? It was called a GI shirt. Oh, Mother! How things have changed. Now guys not only really have armor, but they complain it's not thick enough! Oh, just a little bit of levity. And again it's time for a little comedy relief. My captain—and he really was "my captain," because nobody else gave me orders—knew many other officers, especially company officers, that we called on. And naturally, I got to eat at a lot of different messes. This particular day we were just outside of a big village, Tronia, which was, as everything is in Sicily, on the top of a hill. They claimed cities like this were built on hilltops to help defend them from bandits way back when. This was to be the site of a very tough, ongoing fight, and we were to get up there with our load. But first, the captain said we had business with some heavy-duty artillery outfit at the base of our side of the hill. He said this outfit had just gotten a lot more new 155s, and even two new Piper Cubs for aerial observation. BIG TIME.

Oh yes, I love to see power and lots of it. I love my rifle, and even though it counts, it can only amount to a flake of snow in a storm. But when there's enough flakes, they can stop anything dead, like really dead, as well as the big stuff. Big guns, big ships, and loads of tanks and tank killers, the stuff we need is really beginning to pour in and we're laying it on the enemy just as fast. All this is great, but in the end, you can believe it's the rifle stuck in his mouth that will bring any Bugger to his knees! Sons of bitches!

Oh, hell, I'm forever fighting my memory and my feelings for the lead coming out of this pencil. I know, it's crazy to have such a thought, but what I wouldn't give to get one more crack at it! The thrill of the of the high, super high of adrenalin sharpening your sight, the volume of sound telling you what's coming, your body feeling expanded. I guess it's old age dimming my brains. Never weep for a soldier, not even the dead ones. They have lived, bitching and moaning for sure, but lived on the pinnacle of life, even to the beloved thrill in the enjoyment of taking some other's life in a fire fight. With the old excuse, "I didn't pull my trigger, he did. If I did it, he can blame himself; he made me do it." Oh yeah!

Again, I'll try for the funny story. The captain was to check in with some artillery unit. I can't remember the name or number. There were beginning to be so many of them. As we pulled up and stopped in the road alongside some small planes in a field to our right, a sign over on our left read, Umteen whatever Artillery, with an arrow pointing the way.

I took the captain, as usual, to some command tent. He told me to go get some breakfast. "Gladly, sir, gladly."

I parked out of the way of the kitchen truck and got on line. And what a line I got on. This was an "upscale" outfit; the artillery surely eats better than the "doggies." I smelled coffee, sausages and beautiful PANCAKES! Pancakes—I can't remember the last time; I think it was in Fort Knox, certainly never overseas. The line was getting shorter, the gorgeous smell closer. Then this timid, skinny guy laid two pancakes on me. Oh, what a chance. I said, "Hey, soldier, you guys are sure great cooks. Could I get two more for my poppa?"

He gave me a big smile, and said, "Sure, when you come back!" Oh well, I did try, and I did have two pancakes, a sausage and a canteen cup full of hot coffee. And look at that golden syrup glistening.

As I moved away to find a place to eat . . . oh, I couldn't wait; I hadn't had a breakfast like this since Fort Knox. Of course there were none of the guys squatting around that I knew, so I parked down by a nearby wall. I only got to squat when, whistles, planes. What! Come on, not again! I hovered like a new mother to protect my golden loot. There they were, high over head heading west, some guns firing, but not many. They passed us by, then out of sight over a hill. I thought, *I don't care how high they are; they're going to do that "reverse" stunt again!*

I saw a stone wall, like the kind farmers build. I scrabbled over to it and got on the side of it between me and those disappearing planes. Don't tell me, I know they're going to pull that trick of zooming back. Hunched down against the stone wall, I waited, and waited, coffee getting cold, the sun sparkle dimming off the golden syrup. I gave in. I figured this time I was wrong.

Now, you know, experience counts for a lot. But not when you're stupid, and hungry! I couldn't wait any longer. I got my butt up on the stone wall, coffee on the left, pancakes, sausage on the right. And to stretch out the beauty of the pancakes I decided to sip the coffee first. No lie, just as I was carefully putting that hot metal edge of the canteen cup to my lips, thinking joyful thoughts, Bam! AA guns, whistles, planes.

I didn't get to see the planes. I dove down alongside the wall, thinking, *Damn, what took those bastards so long?* And, *Jeez! Did I hit the mess kit on the way down? Oh no, not the mess kit!*

There were plenty of guns firing this time. At least I had placed myself with the wall between me and them and was sure, as long as they didn't drop bombs, I was safe. In a moment it was all over; they were gone. But, as always, some men hollering, "Medic."

As I got up I saw across the road that one of the small planes was lopsided and burning. I also saw my canteen cup on the ground. But looking around, no pancakes. Hey! They're still up on the wall, great! Nope, guess again. Climbing up on the wall to look over on the other side, forget it! There's the bottom of my mess kit looking at me in the dirt and rocks below. Aw, hell. Then, "Dave! Dave! Come on, we've got to get going." The captain's hot on something.

I didn't tell him I had nothing to eat. I wanted to get going myself before them black-cross Buggers came back for the other small observation Cub that it looks like they had been after too, but had missed.

Boy! I mean, this is a wild life. Just to think, on the ship from the USA, with all the talk, we had hoped the Germans wouldn't give up and leave the place when they found out the Americans were coming. Oh, please, no laughing. Virgins do dream. And in time, usually will find out the hard way. The Germans, far from quitting, were waiting for us. And would give us all a belly full of more adventure and fighting than we ever dreamed of. And never ceased. Whoops! I'm wandering off again.

Now to get back. We were back on the same road of the aborted breakfast, going north. Don't ask me where; that was the captain's job. As long as we were away from those big damn guns. Being near them could compare to riding on the ducks at the shooting gallery. They were always the center of attention. That is attention from the wrong people. The captain was telling me how the Germans were in for a big surprise from this outfit we had just been at because they had just added a lot of new 155s "to help blow the Germans out of Tronia."

As we started around the base of the hill or mountain, whatever it was, to go up the hill to Tronia, I heard behind us, *Wham!* Oh boy, not to worry, it's outgoing. Must be the 155s. Oh yeah! *Wham!* Closer. What the hell? *BaWham!* Right at our backs! *BraDoom!* Right over us. Holy hell! I did my old trick of trying to push the brake pedal through the floor and rip the steering wheel out with my hands.

Stopped, stunned, panting, waiting for the next blow, which came just ahead. *What's? What's?* You can't blame my mind for being spooked when it feels like we're in the path of a runaway train, an enormous, large, giant train! Shaking our heads, I'm thinking that I never would have believed I'd hear anything louder than that navy shell that had ripped over my head, but under the muzzles of these 155s it felt like body blows. The 155s were doing something they never did before, something they couldn't do before. But now they had some fifteen or twenty guns they could work with. They had placed them just at the tree line, covered with camouflage nets, out of sight of the road, and hub to hub they were firing them in sequence over the road and onto the far side of Troina.

Still shaking our heads, holding our ears, looking at the captain I could tell he was very mad, very mad that no one had warned us. Or that his fairy might have let him down, making him worry for once. But then again, he had told me they were getting a lot more guns. Guess they couldn't wait to use them. Still, we were both alive.

I couldn't help thinking what it must have been like on the receiving end. Shells must have come over to them like we had a monster machine gun. Oh yeah! Great! Seldom did I get a laugh thinking of Germans, my Buggers.

Remember I said I'd insert a little levity for comedy relief? Well, I hope you enjoyed my pancake day. I try to put in things, especially nonsense, to cover the fact I'm short of conversations between myself and others. That's because I believe the "banal" never got to enter my memory bank. You know the old saying, "garbage in, garbage out," or something like that. But I have no problem remembering his "Dave! Lets get the hell out of here!"

If I can't remember small conversations, I would have to make them up. If I did that, it could lead to my making up other things, which I don't want to do. If the many times I say I suffered being dived on and flown over by the black crosses seems an extended exaggeration, it is not. I can't possibly remember the amount of times I flipped off that switch (ignition) and baled out to get away from the load, leaving me usually face down in the dirt, heart pounding, and even sometimes biting the dirt, feeling the muscles of my butt over-tightening. It's a feeling of utter, absolute suspense waiting for that tap on your back that you might live to feel. But you know that will be the last you'll ever feel!

I used to think the worst part of the "truck" job was that I never got the chance to shoot back, but now I think (what did I say before about everything being relative?) the truck job saved me from the infantry absolutely. And being "railroaded" into the infantry saved me from the tanks absolutely. Who's to complain?!

Whenever I said I had enough and wanted to go home, fear had nothing to do with it. It was disgust! What next?! I know I'm impatient to give back to those beloved Buggers. Not just a little, but a lot of what they used on us with such consummate skill. Now, with the advent of fighting generals like Patton and the new heavy weapons made for World War II, not World War I, pouring in, that feeling I had at times of being like the guy attacking the windmill was gone. No matter my disgust at times, I always knew we'd bring them down.

They finally did blow the Germans out of Tronia, but that was a terrible battle. We made many ammo trips up to there. I remember on the last trip to make a drop there I had to pull over to the side, close as I could to the edge, to allow a Jeep pulling a long rope with German bodies attached to parts of it to get them down to the road. They were pulling them down off the hill to take them to Graves Registration. The Germans lost a lot of people there.

XI THIRTY-EIGHT DAYS AND NIGHTS

By now we were moving ahead, like we would for the total thirty-eight days and nights it took us to completely clear the island of Germans. Of course I didn't know anything about it at the time, but Tronia had been the hub of the German main line of resistance, and during the time after that I could see the difference. Unbelievably, we hardly ever saw any more German planes. What I did see one time that made me want to jump for joy and holler, fists in the air, "Give it to them, baby, give it to them," was more of my brothers, this time in planes, American planes with those beautiful white stars, attacking something in front of us. They had formed like a vertical Ferris wheel formation, and as each plane reached the nadir of the loop, they let go with everything they had, shooting the hell out of whatever it was on the ground—a stunt worthy of the Black Americans who we found out later were the pilots. Yes sir, Germany, you turned over a hornets nest. Now all those American hornets are coming together. It took time, we were too few at the beginning, but now you'll find we're too many. Look around, we've come alive. Now in the entire USA everyone is coming together, with materials and fighting men; not just rifles, but with battleships, fighter planes, tank killers, anti-aircraft 90mms to put your 88s to shame. We have no need to use crappy mines, but still we have them if needed, and the in-your-face lethal power we now possess.

I know, more endless mental bragging to myself, but it keeps me going. And now, just for a damper, and a big damper, that is, for us—we found out later that the town the American planes had shot up had been in American possession, and all the causalities were ours. Not the fault of the planes, the fault was poor communications. "Friendly fire" again. And to speak about "friendly fire," many men like myself who were grievously wounded by our own side, by mistakes or stupidity, of course, but wounds nevertheless, we were denied because of the Purple Heart rules that are strictly held that wounds must have been administrated by the enemy, which in turn of course means anyone killed or wounded during the attack on the town was ineligible for the award because it was American planes that shot them up! Now, how about that! I shouldn't say it, but it makes me feel a little less bitter. And after all, I did get my chance to make a good "Bugger score." And then I'm sure an even bigger score with my lethal 3/4 Dodge feeding the boys on the line their munitions.

Now, since we weren't worried much about German planes anymore, a lot of stuff, I mean armor, was parked out in the open. And at this field, looking way up from where I was, I could see what we were told was Mount Etna, which of course meant nothing to me except it seemed to be the biggest mountain on the island that I had seen. I can't say for sure, but this happened one time when I had dropped off the captain and was just relaxing, waiting for him. Hey! Just relaxing! I haven't gotten to write that many times! Now again I must emphasize that what I put down is real, nothing made up, and this surely did make an impression on me. I was standing a little away from my empty "bomb." I had my hand on the back of a half-track and was bulling with some guy sitting on its tail, when all of a sudden it felt exactly like I was standing on Fourth Avenue in Brooklyn as a subway train rushed by underneath. It shook everything as it went by. What the hell was that? Believe me, it was great that the Germans were gone. But you still never knew what might happen next.

As my eyes snapped up, looking around, the open landscape around me was undulating like waves at the beach! But slower. Holy Moses! Jeez, what next? How can it do this? What's happening now? Good Christ! And just as I was thinking this, both me and the umpteen-ton half-track went up and down so easily it buckled my knees. I lost my stomach, and it felt like I had just swallowed a gallon of ice water. Earthquake! An earthquake yet? I had never been in an earthquake before. I had never seen solid earth move like Jello.

Several times since then I have read of Mt. Etna erupting, with people being killed in their homes, not just causing an earthquake, but rivers of molten lava as well. The earthquake was enough for me! God and nature can sure make a man's effort to destroy look puny. It was over quick, but remains one of my more lasting memories.

Later on, after we had come up on some place called Rondezo, we were relieved. Activity was reduced almost to standing guard. Now, these are the words exemplifying one of the pure hells of war. To never get a full night's sleep, dead on your feet, but you have to do it. Everyone has to do it. And always fighting off sleep. And while you're pulling the watch, the fear of any sound or sight enhancing your fight to stay alert, not just for yourself now but now for all your buddies as well, finger on the side of the trigger guard, safety off. More strain. The fear of dropping one of your own guys; this and the fact that you can't move around except very slowly. It's movement that can give you away. And it's movement that enemy patrols are watching for. Even with the hard-to-see mouse or deer, it's movement that gives them away. So suffer, and watch each hour go by as if the earth has decided to slow down.

Babbling again. I guess I can mark that down as my dissertation on guard duty. And why to this very day I never wear a wrist watch. Looking at one brings back too many, should I say, unpleasant memories.

Now another story: One afternoon, sitting on a park bench on Shore Road in Brooklyn overlooking the great port of New York Bay, one of my friends was casually flipping a fifty-cent piece, just talking. I noticed one of the girls had her eyes on the piece as it spun; those eyes were attracted and so was she. The gong rang in my head. I want to be able to do that! I'm quitting school. I'm getting a job so I can have money too. You wonder what a shiny fifty-cent piece can do? Back then (1937) it was the same as flipping greenbacks in today's world (2007) of inflated money. I just heard on the TV that by 2009 any person sweeping the floor for one hour must be paid, by law, 7.25. And I guess by 2020 it will be twenty dollars! God help anyone living on a pension.

Anyway, I got a job—my uncles saw to that—at the shipyard. Even though in the days of the Great Depression money was very tight, people did manage to get along. Even at the shipyard the top mechanics worked for ninety-five cents an hour, and as an apprentice I earned thirty-five.

How could you live on that? It wasn't all bad. I could get ham, eggs and coffee for twenty-five, and transportation on trolleys or even a ferry cost only a nickle. So you can see, any guy flipping half-dollars had to be a "right guy" that the bobby-sock girls would cuddle up to. I decided to go to work.

Starting to work in the shipyard presented a little problem—alcohol. The devil from hell who invented that sure got a medal. Here I had a little brush with, as they say, the thief that gets in your mouth and steals your brains.

I had tried alcohol a couple of times at my first job at Bethlehem Steel shipyard in Brooklyn. No cream puffs worked there. Now, before the work hour, it was the custom of many of the big, tough men—believe me, even the smaller guys were tough—to start the day with the prerequisite measure of "mother's milk." That's what they called it. It was a cup of coffee that was half whiskey. The challenge, to me at least, was to throw it down without crying out, gulping, gasping or breaking out in tears, then comment on how great it was, in a muted hoarse voice. Which was not what the others did. They roared approval, pounded the tables and gloried in it. I had to fight not to puke. This shot would make those guys happy, and last most of the day before they ever felt sick. Whereas with me, I never got happy, I just got sick! So even though I never knew at the time how "lucky" I was, and I was never to want any more of it, or the smell of it, I felt unhappy that I couldn't measure up, or, as they say, hold my liquor.

Nevertheless, to work in the shipyard I had to hang tough! You had to be; even "inside" jobs—that's somewhere inside the ship—were tough. Usually the ship's engineer, expecting a trip to the shipyard, would save the worst jobs for the yard men. Under the floor plates of the engine room, above, around and, worse, inside the boilers (asbestos), replacing failed tubes, any and all piping or machinery under the floor plates of the machinery spaces, or the reverse, doing a job on the very top of the masts—lights, radios, etc. How about working on staging over the side of the ship? So cold we worked in alternate twenty-minute shifts. Any carelessness or mistakes, and you could fall in the river, or if the ship was in dry dock, you could get killed falling on the deck.

Working a job on the dry dock under the ship could be the worst. A dry dock consists of a very large, empty tank that has a deck equipped with wooden blocks to accommodate the bottom of a ship. After the tank is filled with water, a ship brought in above will be picked up as the water is pumped out of the tank. When all is in place the dock will be about three or four feet above the level of the river, and the ship itself sitting on the blocks will leave about four feet of clearance between it and the dock for men to work in. Now, where it gets tough is in the winter when large blocks of ice floating or being blown down the river by the wind are inadvertently picked up along with the ship. It takes a man with very tough skin or multiple pairs of long johns to work in a mess like that, which I have done wearing three pairs of gloves (scout's honor)—a dress pair and a leather work pair, both inside a pair of heavy leather welders mitts. Now, of course, as men will, there are times they have to relieve themselves. Urinating isn't bad; you have the whole river to arch a stream into, and need only expose a minimum of skin, standing with your back to the wind. Now then, it really takes a real need, along with guts and stamina to attempt to move your bowls, because this will be a movement you'll never forget. And I say this with certainty, as I have, should we say, been exposed to it. I've never forgotten. Grit your teeth hurrying to the end of the pier, where management has thoughtfully provided a large plank with accommodating holes cut into it, where you can place your bare butt on any hole, upwind or down, to discover it doesn't matter; the wind will tear at you just the same. Just try to beat the world's record for defecating before your scrotum cracks and spills your goods. This is 1937, baby; things are getting better for the working man. I'm told how lucky I am getting to use the newly installed plank. The company didn't have such conveniences before. I guess I can be excused for thinking this is a tough life, because I still was only seventeen.

Another thing, I had three uncles working there. They were Lavertys, my mother's brothers. I'm sure my Dad must have tiptoed around and behaved courting my mom, or he would have had three tough, no I shouldn't say tough, let's say hard guys on him. Back in

Scotland they had all worked in the "Clide," a shipyard, and played on the local football team, with helmets and pads unknown. But not skull fractures. These men, I'm sure they were better prepared than me for this outdoor reliefment (my word) (defecating) than me, coming from a wild, cold country where all, *all* toilet activity was held outside in an air-conditioned shack. Some places, I would guess, to save digging, they would be placed or perched on the edge of cliffs or canyons.

Well, anyway, I felt left out having, at best, failed at assimilating alcohol and also being unable to remain placid moving my bowels while I was contemplating if I was dropping frozen turds or testicles into the river. My only option when I stood up with all the tough guys was to loudly order my milk served in a dirty glass. That'll show them (old Bob Hope joke). Oh, just kidding, but not about the alcohol. I couldn't keep it down.

Now to get back to 1943. The word had spread, I believe by my captain, that on the thirteenth I would turn twenty-one and would now be able to vote for President Roosevelt (Har, Har), who hated war and had proclaimed, "Our boys will never go overseas." But of course that was before things got so bad, especially with France literally joining up with the aggressors. No! Wait! Sorry, no more preaching.

The medics gave me a half a canteen cup full of pure white liquid to sip as we celebrated. Even just sipping shortened my breath. I was to find out later it was 140-proof, pure alcohol. The next thing I remember was an officer kicking my legs, then grabbing hold of my shirt to pull me out from under a truck, yelling at me how I could have been killed! Oh, please, sir, do you see my head anywhere under there?

Now that I was twenty-one and smart enough to know if being stupid and unfettered, feeling free to lose your mind, brains and good health to such cheer, count me out. I can be tough enough without any "aqua vita." (That's Latin for "water of life," or whiskey.)

See how smart I iz? Now you've learned something today. Maybe you can tell by my writing that I'm being silly. The pressure is off with no more wondering what hell is going to pop up next. With them Buggers gone, it's relaxing time. Let some levity sneak in. Just keep out of trouble, and maybe, after all, you might make it home.

Shortly after that the entire First Division fell back to the beaches we had conquered, Gela and Licata. Going back down to the southern part of the island was just following a trail of destruction. All of the dead had been buried, and I had to wonder what they had done with all the dead horses. Lord, how they stank. Horses are big, and the stink matches their size. The so-called "motorized" German Army certainly used enough of them. And all kinds of odd-shaped wagons, or I should say, splintered wagons.

We had many detours around blown bridges. And some of the towns we passed through had a really bad smell from the many people buried in the rubble. The bombers and the artillery had done that. I remember the day we saw the first heavy bombers going overhead we knew we had it made. That day, everyone stopped doing whatever they were at, and all were looking up at what sounded like a swarm of bees of in the distance. Then louder, like a buzz saw. Bombers, big bombers, and them big, beautiful white stars on them. Thank God! Most everyone went hoarse yelling themselves crazy, jumping up and down, waving as if they could be seen. Who cares? Those are our boys up there, not black crosses! Mr. German, do we have enough brothers now?! But they're only the little brothers; the bigger boys are still on the way. And this proved to be no empty brag!

Shortly after they passed overhead we heard a great rumbling and you could actually feel the ground shake We wondered how anyone could stand up to that. We had been bombed, panicked and scared, but never anything like that! Well, great! And don't weep for them; they started something, half-assed, king of the world crap. Now they will suffer. Tough shit on the Germans.

We had conquered Africa and Sicily, and now we had to get all our gear, especially vehicles, ready for the big parade at home. We were told to wash the vehicles with a mixture of gasoline and oil to make the olive drab shine like new. You don't want your mom or dad or sweetheart to think we're a bunch of bums. Oh, come on! There's the bullshit again—all that talk about going home. And again, I would like to apologize if I write in a way that makes me some kind of oracle or genius, but as I have said before, that's the way it comes out some-times. I told anyone willing to listen that this was against logic. We're now the best fighting men in our army, and all of the "fingers" of the First Division have now come together creating a mighty fist. We're not here on an outing. We're here for a purpose. And now we've got the fist to do it. We're going to punch our way right up through Italy and into Hitler's ass. When it's over, we'll go home.

I'm sorry. I hate to shoot down anyone's balloons, but you're part of the First Infantry Division, the division that's paid a heavy price to be taught by the German Army how to fight "their" way, and by giving it a little extra effort, we can improve on it. We owe it to all those guys we lost getting here.

Now, what I have just written is my mind. My mind's thinking of that time back then, written as is, not a copy, no erasures, just the way it came out of my head through the lead of the pencil. Maybe boring or repetitious, but unvarnished. Remember, at the time I was not a person! I was a soldier. And I despised. No, wait, that's too strong a word; let's just say I didn't care for anyone who didn't wear my uniform. And I think my greatest irritation were crybabies. I've always hated crybabies. No, don't say, "hate." Save hate for the enemy; just say, "disliked." Of course, I can't swear those are my exact words. My pencil or memory isn't that good. And also, I've toned it down for the ladies. Levity? Sure. Enjoy! Enjoy!

Later on, after I had carried out some kind of errand for the captain, I found myself driving back along the blacktop road that ran parallel to the beach off Gela, site of my beloved Blue Beach, where the rusted hull of the destroyed landing ship, 313, still sat firmly in like a pit of sand. I came to the place where the captain and I had crossed coming up from the beach the second time, that is, with the major who wanted to reconnoiter like we were going for a drive back in Kentucky or being escorted by some heavily armed protection, of which there had been none. This was it. I recognized the two peculiar sand dunes with the partial grass patches that I had so desperately tried to get back to on foot, knowing absolutely I'd never make it. Never! It's hard to believe that all of my courage and determination had melted into piss-filled pants and trembling, gutless flesh. If those bastards are not just after me, they are sure making me think so!

That was then, now only a teeth gritting memory. But this spot was real to me. Yes, this was the spot. Real quiet now, but by looking out along the anti-tank ditch I could see the bits and pieces of shapeless scrap where the navy had torn up the landscape, squeezing my heart into the size of a gnat, then bursting with power when I realized what was happening. But up until then, at the peak of my fright, I had been damning the Dragon for saving me for this. Again! Running without a weapon. Then the thunderclap of a huge navy shell, its passage over me alone almost lifting me off the ground, coming so close.

Of course I know, like anyone else, the enemy coming at me is after the invading army, not just me. But somehow, face down in the sand, you get the feeling of rage that they're doing this just to get at you. I'm sure other individuals must have at times felt this. Then knowing, *I'm going to get to feel what it's like now! But Christ, what in the hell are they firing at me now? It feels like explosions right over me, pressing me into the sand, not shells.*

In my rage I lifted up to turn my head and get in one last defiant yell and shake of my fist before I was surely to be run over. Damn! Another blast! And another, and another! Holy hell. Uncomprehending, my squinting eyes discerned a difference. It wasn't me, it was them! The tremendous blasts were coming from the sea! The navy! Our navy! Hell's fire! Thinking only of our Cannon Company, forgetting the navy. We never had a navy back us up before. It's giving the reprieve to me and hell to the enemy. My relief so boundless, laughing, laughing, and at the time screaming with joy. I had jumped up, howling and dancing with glee in the sand that had held my fearful, scrunching body just seconds before. All this before I thought that I'd better get down before a navy shell took my head off.

Then I remember looking way down on the side of the tank ditch. And there, impervious to all, sat the truck. Impossible! What a sight!

Now today, standing here in this puddle of memory, writing of events that rained on me here. You may think I wrote too much about it. I tell you, I didn't write enough! The whole experience now reminds me of, say, after watching a violent movie, like King Kong tearing New York apart, in the theater when I was a kid, then stepping outside to the peace and quiet of normal life. You're instantly shorn of the excitement of the beast coming at you, and you tumbled back down to your boring life. Oddly, these were my feelings. Here I was again, and looking around it was so peaceful, so quiet, with only the murmur of my truck's engine. Could all that have been real? Or just a bad dream? No, looking around, no matter the deception of peace and quiet, there were pieces of scrap here and there telling of a recent violent moment in time. My eyes and my mind taking in a violence that was really only the opening orchestration, a preview to the about-to-begin main play—the freeing of Europe, and the destruction of the Germans! It has just started. Oh yeah!

On returning to the beach, it felt strange not to be always on the alert and on guard, which I had been ever since those hills in Africa. Now, here in the peace of the Germans gone, you could still see the blown-up "beach houses" and "bungalows" that had been heavily reinforced concrete bunkers, tank bodies and displaced guns, wreckage still strung out along the beach, and the very unhappy sight of the LST 313. The big bow doors had been removed as salvage for some other damaged LST, I guess. With the gaping, open front you could see all of the insides, the sun shining through all the holes and sections blown away in the deck above from the fire and explosions following the bombing. The burned wreckage of our cannon company's Jeeps, trucks, guns, half-tracks, etc., were still standing on the upper and lower decks.

Here on the beach, staring out at this tremendous amount of destroyed equipment sitting dead in the now-peaceful rippling surf, I'm rooted to the spot. Not trying to be poetic, but I have to speak the anguish I feel in my mind, the mind I keep trying to describe to you. The thought of all those men and their possessions, their inevitable pictures of home, parents and girls, all destroyed, left an impression on the mind of a young guy brought up in the Depression, where a five-dollar bill could mean a day at Coney Island with rides and treats, kissing and hugging your girl on the giant Ferris Wheel. And be sure to always get her on the sliding, swinging car of the Ferris Wheel, because when that car reaches the apex of the wheel, it swings out to her screaming. It's designed to scare her, as well as me, so that she would squeal and hug you tight. Oh, man!

At the moment my mind is just bathing in the memory. It can make an old man weep. That is of today (2007), but to go back, look at what's been lost! How many five-dollar bills did it take to make the mess I'm looking at? And I'm only looking at the front of it. The rusted carnage extends all the way back through the entire length of this destroyed ship and, no doubt, contains many undiscovered bodies, bodies that many parents spent many more than five dollars to raise. Nothing but a torn up hull and ashes, bitter ashes. And still, we must be ready to go again, and again, until this damnation is resolved, and every young man is free to taste his love of life before falling into the inevitability of the ravages of old age and living on nothing but memories.

Again I must apologize. I couldn't help it. It all poured out of my pencil. But anyway, with all these little interruptions, they must clue you in on my feelings. True feelings. Nothing made-up or imagined at a later date than the memory of the mess I face now! Remember, it is my mind I'm writing about; it's a little bent for sure, skating on a layer distorted by hate, but I can still focus, doing my job.

Now, I had heard you could buy ice cream in Licata, another town nearby. What I found was a guy selling shaved ice with different flavors. It wasn't bad, still a treat, but what I also found, and what was to lead me down the garden path, as they say, was an engineer. Notice: drivers wanted to pick up abandoned enemy equipment. Wow! Guns, knives, flags, etc., and a chance to get away from all the crappy details. I'm afraid my logic wasn't working that day. If all those goodies were laying around, why would they have to advertise? Forgetting the oldest rule of survival in the army: Never, never, never volunteer in the army. I volunteered! My only excuse—extenuating circumstances. (Now there is a mouthful of words.) I wanted to get away from all the "chicken" details. I don't mind working hard when there's a purpose, but keeping me busy to keep me out of trouble is a drag.

It turned out they weren't lying. It really was abandoned enemy equipment. The gag was, it was all in artillery shells, bunkered along roads, anywhere there was some overhead vegetation. This was, of course, to limit destruction of any force brought against them to the immediate area. Now what's that word again? Touché. I think that's French for balls! Well, I was committed. Hell, it couldn't last for too long, anyway. And it didn't! My Dragon or Dragons tired of me and presented their bill, not to be paid in full, by death, but as a longtime payment in anguish, unbelievably for over sixty tears.

Now, if you will go back to the beginning of my story, you'll know how my sojourn came to an abrupt end. Hell, sojourn only means temporary visit anyway—temporary visit to a mad house lasting seven months combat time, or was it seven years? And looking back on it, I have to admit it was in the reality of the unmentionable. The mental organism of killing men and endlessly ducking death by both accident and design. That easily puts the first night of marriage, as a comparison, in the shade! Marriage involves love, whereas war involves hate! A burning, consuming fire in the mind. The inexplicable drive to "get" before you're "gotten." I always was aware, or at least assumed, the Dragon would not give free rides forever, and sooner or later I'd get a bill. A quick one, I hoped. But it wasn't to be. Instead I got it in an installment for over sixty years. . . . And here's how I remember it started—in the Seventy-Seventh Evacuation Hospital in Sicily.

Be advised, I cannot swear to the truth of all that follows. My mind for some time, to say the least, seemed disoriented. I learned in time to ignore things like, how did I get here? I was laying in a cot; I could feel the sticks on either side of it. Yes, I can. "I" was; who's "I?" I'm thinking, *David? I'm David. I'm finally dead. No, I can't be. I still see daylight. But I'm laying in a cot; there's not a sound. Yes there is; someone is humming. My head feels like it's laying on the housing of an electric motor that's running. How did I get here? Hey, look, there's a pretty girl. Oh, that's too bad; she has two heads. But the heads are smiling at me. No, that's not it. It's not her; it's me. Everything is double; I must have double-vision. I see her lips are moving, but nothing's coming out. I'm not sure, I'm going to slip back to where I was. Yeah, that's better. I feel something cold and wet on my head, nice.*

This is the way I remember, the way I made it back. The gap between my putting the writing pad on the steering wheel and my mind coming back into focus, the fear and desperation of trying to climb the wall, trying to shake off the weight on my back, to what the hell had happened? Finally guys, good guys, helping me. Helping me to do what? Oh yes, to get me over the wall. Then, somehow they got me in this tent. And I'm laying in the comfort of the cot. Time? I don't know anything about time. But in time I got all of my faculties to come back. Even my peace of mind. A lot of happy, laughing people, after a while they came through the tent. It was Bob Hope and his entourage. (That means accompanied by pretty girls) I remember him and a movie star named Adolf Monjou. Bob Hope didn't come down my side of the tent to speak to me, but Adolf did. Coming down my side of the tent, he said, "Hey, soldier, got a match?" Sure it was a joke, for all to see. I was in no position to give anyone anything. It was nice, just fun.

Again I feel I must remind that this is not a made-up story; no matter, it is to the best of my ability, even if at times it may be boring or redundant, it is to the best of my ability true! Sometimes I can't believe it myself.

The continual humming and whistling in my head was unpleasant. But the pretty nurses were very pleasant, and it was even more of a treat to see American girls. There's nothing like seeing your own kind of girls. Whatever memory I have comes in spurts and blanks. I remember being happy and sad. I'm told I'm to be sent to a hospital in England. *But, Dad* (Oh, I'm just talkin in my head to my dad) *I did get in my "bite." Now others must take over.*

Right now I feel like I've fallen off the roof. I'm like busted inside. Maybe with some luck I'll be back with the captain. I don't want to be dealt out of the fight so soon. We've got a long way to go. And even better good news—all of the First Division is to be sent back to England.

XII

My next big memory, I was on the biggest ship ever. It was a British transport, but searching my mind I can't for the life of me remember how I got from the evacuation tent of the hospital to the ship. It must be true, I can only remember things that impressed me. Fortunately, I wasn't going to England alone, although again the captain, I mean Captain Kendal, was on another ship. It would seem he was important enough to travel only on ships with beds, not bunks. My ship was a fine, accommodating British transport. I did have the company of my other guys; in fact, I was told it was taking most of the entire First Infantry Division back to England. Unfortunately, as you can guess, it did not have American food.

Now, of course, armies must always act in inscrutable ways. We were told that somehow the British soldiers were loaded on American transports; that's so they could eat our grub while we ate there's. I do believe, no one got fat on our trip to England. I can't say how the British fared on ours, but none of us cared for theirs. It was composed mainly of salmon and/or ground-up dog meat (corned beef), complete with bones, hair and enough fat—I mean real, looking at you, yellowish fat—to make the lumps go down (ox tails). I understand they also used this spread on the launch blocks to slide ships into the water. And that lip-smacking treat, "Bully Beef." It's made of mangled beef compressed into a can, no doubt with at least part of the cow's asshole included to give it that everlasting flavor! I know I shouldn't say such things, but a guy can't help what he's thinking. To us American soldiers, the food was awful. That's putting it mildly.

There are two meals I can remember still. One was there standing in a can—a large, tall can I admit, but hardly enough to feed three hungry young men—containing some kind of strong, smelly dead salmon. The smell permeated the air. No wonder each can could stand up with the roll of the ship; the smell was that strong. Four cans on a table for twelve men. And the other meal I remember was getting the great deceiver, platters of sliced meat. Yum, yum! Gorgeous, beautiful, delicious-looking, at last! Unbelievable, and it was! This looked great and smelled great, and then we also learned another new word, mutton. We found out this meat is not meant to eat, it's meant to resole boots. Or it certainly could be. It's got to be an art to make a piece of meat that tough. And then to top it all off. Another new word, marmalade. Candied orange skins. What man could handle such delicacies? Think of it, candying garbage. What a shame, all these years at home throwing away the skins!

Back home I had heard of guys smoking banana skins, but never heard of any use for bitter, bruised orange skins. I know, it's all sarcasm, but it does help level anger and frustration. And it helped make the grubby-looking port of Liverpool look great. Where's the gangway? Where do I get off? I suppose it's normal that men of different countries eat many different types of food—the British with their ox-tail soup, with, of course, part of the tail hair and bones included. I'm not being funny, it's the truth. There's a piece of the end of tail, hair and bones meticulously packed in each can. Why do they can the bones? "Why, chum, that's in case you're hungry, they're to suck on when you finish the soup."

I really got that answer from a guy (British), and he also said, "Such a silly question. You Yanks are certainly odd. You wouldn't throw away the bones, would you?"

Oh, good heavens, no.

How about the Italian munching on raw onions. Not to forget the Germans. Have you ever tried a can of their omnipresent sardines? They have so many bones, it's like eating some kind of smelly grit, or fish-flavored sand. It's a wonder they don't wear out their teeth. Not to forget those used condoms of blood pudding. Or at least that's the way they come. And with such a disgusting look. Ugh! And the winner at fighting digestion—English tea that comes in a can with ground-up, shredded tea leaves and dehydrated donkey milk, all included together.

I asked another guy, this time a limey, "How do you drink tea like that without choking?"

"No problem, chum, as you sip it, keep your teeth shut tight."

Why, of course! Why didn't I think of that?!

I guess that's enough sarcasm. Well, anyway, it keeps your mind off being hungry!

One night on board after I had finished what supper had been served, I hadn't been feeling to good, so I didn't get exposed enough to the "goodies" to make me want to throw up. I just wanted to get some fresh air and peace after, if you will pardon the expression, "supper" was over. It seemed like every guy inside that had been issued cigarettes was chain smoking like he was being paid money to do it and trying to out-yell each other while they played cards. So I went out on deck.

I stepped into the darkness, lit only by the bright silver radiance overhead of the trillions of stars that could not only be seen but felt. As the beams of the myriad lights came down, they massaged your body vertically, while the cool sea breeze in turn came along horizontally to pleasure your body with fresh rippled air. The feeling was almost like stepping into a new body and being massaged into a different "fairy" dimension. To be on a blacked out ship on a black ocean on a black night with no moon, with just the sight of the "Disneyland" of stars, overwhelmed any thoughts in my head. Stretching out on a hatch cover in the quiet hissing of the ship's progress, I relaxed into a mental mood, my mind aboard a space ship zooming up to the shoals of stars, drinking in the myriads of sparkling diamonds marking the outermost reaches of space—a sight impossible for anyone to see on land or even on a ship that's not blacked out. Here on the ocean, on a moonless night far from any shore lights to dissipate the view, I feel contentment. I feel the gray stuff in my skull reaching out to the canopy above, longing to be embraced in its perpetual glory, feeling, as it were, my being a speck, for whatever reason, a tiny intelligent speck among the billions, trillions, uncountable similar specks in the universe. And wonder why?

Laying back on the cover of the forward hatch, assuming my favorite position, arms and hands behind my head, I unhappily, inadvertently reminded myself of the last time I did this, on the beach in Sicily. It was when I was just in time to catch the despicable destruction wrought by the dive bomber. It was certainly the opposite of this comforting sight of drinking in the beauty of the universe spilling into my eyes. How could anything of this magnitude be confined to a single religion? What religion could possibly pretend to encompass the immensity of our universe? Is it because its vastness is not normally seen as I see it now? Seeing the infinity of space from a darkened ship, how can anyone, holy or professing the same, reduce this image to the image of a single man? An A-rab dressed man, holy man, walking, *walking* among the declared sinful people, spending his time amusing them with tricks and miracles.

Indisputably, the power, especially of the blazing sun, is there for all to see every day, pulsating the message of, "Here I am. In time return to me." I'm sure this is not our deity; this is only the radiance of the power we're not allowed to look upon. I maintain that the sun is not the base of our energy or the source of our lives; it is only the holy grail in heaven that we see. The radiance emanating from our living God, available even to the blind, as they are touched by its permeating warmth. Doubt me? How long would anyone or anything live without it? You think I know damn little! I tell you, I know damn all! Oh, just to finishing with a jest. So there.

Other thoughts drifted through my head as well lying here, a wreck of my former self, about how I had wanted to be a soldier, and a tough one, so I could measure up. And did I ever get my wish. I didn't simply go through the fire; hell, I was tossed into the furnace! Now I'm a hard nut. You might say, a cracked hard nut. Rest and rehabilitation, that's what I need, and that's what I'm getting. My main thought right now is that I'll be in good enough shape to go with the boys when we hit on Germany. I'm looking forward especially to going through and over France, excusing ourselves by requesting Frenchmen to stand aside and watch some real men fight! But right now all I have to do is live life smooth and effortless, as the clean ocean breeze that blows over me.

And as the good British ship throbs ahead for its beloved England . . . hey! Now my noisy buddies are spilling out on deck with all their noisy oohs and ahs about heaven, breaking my reverie. As I have said before, army life isn't all bad, as long as you look sharp, listen and don't volunteer! Don't volunteer! Don't volunteer! Oh yeah!

We finally, despite all the submarine scares, arrived in England. I don't remember anything about leaving the ship and getting to a camp, but I do remember we were camped in a row of small English houses. Each one had a fireplace in the corner of the main room, and nowhere else! Englishmen are certainly a perverse group. With the fire in one corner of the room, it didn't take a rocket scientist, or some shivering GIs, to figure out that the rest of the room, not to mention the rest of the house, was poorly served, with the heat, what there was of it, going up the chimney while the smoke came into the room! Better still, the limey in charge of caring for the property, that old fart, he called us fags for needing central heating. And how about the milkman, another sweet old dear? He sold us milk for ten shillings a pop after telling us a shilling in our money was worth a penny. Oh yeah! It took a while to find out that it came to two dollars a bottle. Was it because, as he said, he liked us Yanks? Or was it our money? Anyway, I hope he made enough to retire, because he lost out after we were told there would be a fifty-dollar fine for drinking milk in this country because they didn't inoculate their cows. We had the same fifty-dollar fine in Italy for eating their spaghetti, but we didn't need a fine not to eat it that after seeing how they dried spaghetti. If nothing else, it was simple—by laying it on old newspaper. Of course, not to get the spaghetti dirty, they laid the papers in the dirt in front of their, if you'll excuse the expression, "home," and then let the flies have a ball stamping it dry. Believe me, this is not unearned sarcasm; it's the truth. Also, many of the girls in Italy that looked so good at night were horrors in the daytime—festering sores all over their bodies like tiny pizzas. We were told this came from sleeping with their animals at night for warmth.

All of this was truly just a rest before the training started again. It wouldn't last long. Quiet never lasted long in the army, and it didn't last long for me. All drivers were to report to transportation. We were being sent to pick up new equipment. Now, this part I could never forget. That mighty fist I claimed many times was coming. It was here!

Preparation

Out in the open, spread endlessly, incredibly endlessly, after arriving from cargo-filled ships giving us the might and means for making war, we drove past the front ends of 6 x 6s, the ones at the heads of a line, passing line after line going back out of sight. Then the same with the fronts of light tanks, and Sherman tanks, half-tracks, scout cars, ambulances, artillery, big and small, hundreds of huge wooden crates (we were told held gliders), each line going back in the distance out of sight! Lord, love a duck! Literally mountains of rations, small arms, shells, even some kind of flotation gear for building bridges. We drove past the fronts of ambulances, then more scout cars, then again light tanks, more Shermans with crates strapped on their backs, spare parts for each tank. "God damn!" I had to yell it. He's here; I knew it. My big, biggest Brother is here. Look at that stuff! What could all this possibly cost? If only the Buggers could see what's coming at them from that fuse they lit under us. They'd say their prayers. No wonder they say the barrage balloons are up there to hold the British island up.

As we stopped at a line and drove down alongside it, they dropped a man off at each new truck, then half-track, scout cars, as we went along. I drew a 6 x 6. We had been given a lecture beforehand to positively not at any time drive on the right. On the English roads always keep left. It was an odd feeling, and seemed simple, but really required attention.

All I remember next is getting back to our bivouac. I seemed to be stuck to the seat and felt that feeling again of having no insides and unable to lift my arms. Very unpleasant. Guys helped me out. My pants and the seat were all bloody. And off again I went to the hospital, feeling sure this time I had run out my string. To think, to imagine, I'm going to die in a bed. Soldiers are not supposed to do that. "No!" I remember yelling. "No!" shaking my fist at the ceiling, "I'm still here, you people!" I didn't care who heard me or looked at me.

Sure, it seems silly now, but at the time I really needed a buddy, a Solan, a Captain, to give me a punch on the arm and an "Atta baby, Dave, you're doing great!" Sure! Sure! Languishing in a sack, shrugging off endless tests, probes and questions, like one came from a major. He said he was a psychiatrist and wanted to know if I had killed any of the enemy. And how did I feel about it? He was writing a book to help new men get over the shock of taking a life. I just said, as I remember, in no way being a smart ass or wise guy, only what popped in my head. "My reflex would be, if my own brother took a shot at me and missed, I'd kill him. No regrets. Because he would have been the cause of my pulling my trigger!" Later I found out many veterans used that excuse. You had to. When that weapon in your hand barked, and you could see the result, you were exulted, screaming joy! Afterwards, not then but afterwards, contemplating, you were still never sorry, but didn't think to use it as a brag.

One day—it was one of those ten or fifteen days of the year when people get to see the sun shining in England (Har! Har!)—I had been marked "ambulatory," which meant I could walk around the grounds in my red pajamas marked "Property U.S. Army." As I tiptoed around with a cane, I saw a train go by. I had never seen an English steam engine puffing around before; it was an odd, noisy thing. (You'll think what I'm about to write is like something I read in a humorous newspaper item. But it's not. I actually did this! Sometimes embarrassing, but dammit, I'm only telling the truth, so here. Still makes me shiver writing about it.) I started limping over to get a better look at the tracks. As I did this I saw wood boards nailed lopsidedly around a square hole dug in the ground, like would be done by boys. But when I went over to it I could see it was quite deep and had a homemade ladder in it. And at the bottom there was like a big old tank of water, oil or maybe steam for the weird engine or whatever. I couldn't see any connections. My curiosity was aroused. The tank seemed to be leaning a bit in the hole dug for it. As I looked down, my foot hit a small cross shaped out of two pieces of wood; it went into the hole and with a thud bounced off the tank. With the thud, my mind said, *Hmm, it's full. If it had been empty the wood hitting would have made it ring.* Very observant, yeah ,very observant, but you have to believe I had nothing to think with that day. Who wanted to think anyway? I was just moping around, but mainly my brains weren't in gear.

Holding on tightly to each rung of the ladder in case one of the homemade rungs would break under my foot, I managed to get down. The "thing" or tank, whatever it was, wasn't straight. I just kept, you could say, getting curiouser and curiouser, wondering if I could push it over. As I did, I stepped on the wooden cross at my feet that I had kicked down. I picked it up to toss it out of my way. Oh, my God! Oh, great God! The hand printing, in dripping black letters, froze my eyeballs, brain, guts and rectum: UNEXPLODED BOMB. It turned me into a quivering statue. Yeah, yeah, it sure does look like that. Holy hell.

Not daring to move, still clutching the wood, shaking, unable to stop, my eyes riveted to the metal thing, thinking that I was about to push the damned thing, galvanized me. My mind cleared in a zero second. *Get going, feet and hands, grab on, speedo, speedo.* But I was already too late. What? Listen! A train! A rattling, noisy train! Oh, no, I'll never be able to get up the ladder in time. I remember this clearly. Who wouldn't? I can't really say exactly what I did, but I could see this thing, the bomb, what there was of it, was as big as me, and probably the other buried half was bigger! And it seemed to have expanded in size since I first looked at it. I turned, gripping the wood of the ladder, thinking, *If this goes off I'll be marked down as a deserter, cause they'll never find so much as a fingernail of me.*

Now, I would like to add here that as I write this I can remember the absolute panic, the feeling of trying to breathe in gulps. I wanted to run up the ladder, but didn't dare. Don't shake anything more than that damn engine is going to shake it. But you, that is, the reader, can't feel that because you know I made it, so what's the big deal.

With my hands on the ladder, pressing my forehead against a rung, I waited, not trying to climb. Why waste time? Its good-bye, Mother, again! Head against the lower rung, here it comes! The crappy *whoof, whoof, whoof* of the engine, like the wheezing damn thing was climbing a hill. What hill? All we got is flat, muddy ground here. The slight vibration of it in the ground under my slippered feet seemed to ripple up the insides of my legs and shake the contents of my scrotum, like they were frozen and clinking together unpleasantly. I held tight and scrunched up as it clumsily rattled passed. It had me all but wet my leg. *David! David! You unbelievable dumb bastard, go easy, but get out of here! Get out of this damn hole! Look up there, the blue sky above. Easy now, but GO!*

Getting out, I just went. I had no place in mind; I just went back to the hospital and into the office. I asked the "deary on duty" (because all the English women called us "deary") if that was really a big bomb, and if it was, why would they go away and leave it exposed like that? "Oh yes, deary," she said, "it's a very big bomb and they are going to work on it this Sunday when there's less rail traffic."

Or, I could only think, maybe there'll be less hospital! It will give them more room to work. It's a wonder those bomb removal guys have room to work in that hole with those giant balls they must have! Well, telling you true, I would rather fight than face the paralyzing fright of an unexploded bomb.

Oh yes, that stupidity of mine really left an impression on me. Snapped my addled mind awake, swimming out from under the influence of all those "pain" pills they give me. To think, I had my nose up against the damndest, biggest, probably ticking German bomb ever. I would have been vaporized!

It would seem that now, being more or less out of the fighting, I'm beginning to fear being killed! I can't see why. Or maybe I do. It's the fact that I'm like a woman or a child. I'm defenseless. I have no way to hit back.

I should be fairly safe, but it seems even laying in a bed in an "American" hospital, that is, an American hospital in England, my life is never a drag. (It's not a building; it's a put-together row of Quonset huts. They're separate but linked together by duck boards, including the mess hall. These boards are needed to keep feet and slippers out of the eternal mess created by the incessant rain and drizzle.) So, as I was saying, I'm laying in bed, and it's getting dark. They have closed the windows and installed some clumsy wooden shutters, as they do each night, to cover the windows. As a thought, I asked the guy in the bed next to me, "Why the hell do they wrestle with wood over the windows? Don't they have any curtains?"

He just looked at me, wiggled his finger and gave a big, "Ha!" And turning away from me mumbled, "You'll find out."

What? What's with you, you dumb jerk! What fell on him?

My attention went to the two potbelly stoves in the aisle. Again, more Stone Age equipment, potbelly stoves heating the place. How can England be so far behind us? I wonder, have they invented sliced white bread yet? No, I didn't think that up; it's an old joke, poking fun at the slow country people. Jeez, in a way it's kinda good rural fun. Whenever you want to, you can pick up a piece of coal, open the little door, and throw it in, wondering if it will do any good. Or should I say, "It shouldn't do any harm"—Jewish expression, but on the mark!

It would seem that there are no *mild* potbelly stoves. If you stand close, it will burn you. And if you stand a little away, you can hardly feel anything. Oh, I'm sorry, seems I can't stop razzing the limeys. You're forgetting, you're in a nice comfy bed, relax. War? What war? I'm sure my Dragon has given me up, but still now and then twitches his tail for me. Who in the hell would think those German bastards were still after me?

There was a tremendous *Baharoom, Boom! BaDam* outside. Not too close, but close enough to shake everything in the joint. "Man, say a prayer; some poor bastard like one of those bomb guys, I guess, must have bought it," I said, thinking it was like another accident with munitions.

"Oh no, laughing boy," the nut next to me says. "Now you know why there's wood in the window. Saves the glass. Ah-ha-ha!" And he gives me another of his big "nothing" laughs, then exclaims, wide-eyed, waving his hand, "Buzzz bombs, baby, buzzz bombs."

Holy jeez, wadya know, I gotta get a bed next to a flip bucking for a Section Eight. (That's a discharge for being looney.) *Oh wow*, I wonder, *how long has this guy been confined to that bed?* He didn't make me laugh, because I'm pissed. Buzz bombs back here, or over here, or wherever the hell I am. How many more threats to my life am I going to be able to step between? *Dragon, you dirty, ugly bastard, let's not have any more of this! You're wasting your time. I'm worn out.*

Later, not that day, but some time later, I remember the nurse found my pajama bottoms filled with blood, so they eventually moved me to another hospital, this one in a building like a real back-home hospital. I'm really feeling cared for.

Now something not so funny. I learned a new word—proctology. A rectum examination, and I swear this guy, another major, seemed to enjoy doing it. Now, this is not only painful, it's humiliating as well. As he sticks in a pipe and pumps air up your poop he seems fully engrossed. And mumbling to himself. Oh, what I wouldn't give to be able to give it back. Only a dream, but a dream that eventually came true! I didn't get to do it, but I got to enjoy it!

Seems one morning the going-off nurse gave the wrong man the enema, but the coming-on nurse got the right man for the doctor. He got the guy on the table, on his knees, butt in the air, pipe inserted, and the doctor started to pump the air in for another of his mornings of fun. And when the bowels were full with compressed air, that hairy ass blew all the goulash with whatever else he had eaten the night before into the open mouth and face of the doctor. Not just on the doctor, but all over his office, and the screaming nurse. The yelling and hollering was only drowned out by the gales of laughter, of which I'm sure mine was the loudest.

I'm sure that forever after that the first thing the doc would ask any guy entering his office would be, "Have you had your enema?"

Another morning, again with a nurse. She had just stepped up to me when her eyes went wide. "Oh, Mr. Lawrie, you just stay still. I've got to get the doctor."

"What was that all about?" I asked the guy in the next bed (a normal guy). "What do you think bit her in the ass?" I laughed.

Another guy looking at me said, "Holy hell, what happened to you?"

To make a long story short, one of my blood transfusions, it seems, was bad. It gave me hepatitis B, turning my skin and eyeballs yellow. This in turn forced them to have me lay on a board for seven days. In a private room yet! Away from it all. Seems it's very contagious. There was another guy in a room across from me in the same condition. He taught me how to play Battleship. The nurses would give us graph paper to lay out our fleets, and we would holler our shots back and forth.

In time, another thing they found wrong with me was that while in Italy I had drunk the water instead of the vino. This gave me amoebic dysentery and colitis, not to mention malaria. Imagine! I couldn't catch a bullet, but I caught all these stinking old-world diseases. I finally got out of the room and on my feet. But feeling woozy from past shots, and tired, I was just sitting. And again a nurse lit my fuse, only this time for the greatest ride of my life. She said, "Mr. Lawrie, you're to report to the clothing room to get dressed, and then go out-side in the front of the building and wait for instructions."

I said, "Instructions? You're dumping me out just like that? Oh, just joking, miss; I'll really be glad to get back to my outfit and away from all these doctors."

"Oh no," she said, "you're to be ZI'd."

"What!? What?" I said. "You mean ZI'd, like zone of interior? Isn't that army talk for U.S.A.?" My heart jumped. *It can't be. Aw, another mix up.* I know I'd been sick, passing blood from both ends at different times, not able to eat, but it never entered my mind that they'd send me home.

She said, "No, sir! I saw your chart; you're not going back to war. You're going home. The officer in charge will explain."

Going home. In my mind I remember I couldn't untangle what she said. And I can't honestly to this day remember all the words ,but I had to fill in some of my own just now to explain this move a little. I couldn't believe it . But the elation of going home bit deep. In defense of my being ready to quit, I thought, if it could be, I don't mind. I have ridden enough times on the Dragon's back, scared at times, exhilarated out of my mind in others. Been roughed up enough, tossed aside, quivering in fear, or raging to fight enough times. Got Buggers more than enough. Two months of intermittent fighting or patrols, digging foxholes, standing guard (line company) and playing target for an enemy endlessly trying to kill me. Let new guys try it for a while. When you're new, you can take it more, that is, having people trying to kill you. Then, of course, I got the "tit" job of only having to run explosive "necessary equipment" up to the front lines under fire. At least that would never have wounded me, not even a fingernail. But it was rewarding, knowing how I was contributing.

Still standing dazed in front of the hospital building, I was given a helmet and told to get in the van. What? Oh yeah, it sure looks like I'm being sent home! In a pig's ass. Forget it. What the hell's the helmet for, so I can bring home a souvenir? And then, in the middle of my bitching (to myself), another one of my miracles. Listen, really, it pays to bitch, even mentally. A doctor sticks his head inside the van and tells us, "I suppose you all know you're being flown back to the States for better care." *We* all know?

XIII

We all know? What's today? April first? Oh, come on now! It must be the pills. The humming in my head is getting louder. What am I hearing? First the ZI bit, then the helmet, now flying? Christ, what next? They're certainly not things that fit together! I would just like to go back to my bed and lay down. I'm tired. Instead, true enough, they took us to an airfield. If I remember correctly, it was the Liverpool Airdrome. The British sure have odd names for things. Liverpool. I can understand the pool part; it's a seaport. But Liver? How did that get in there? Looking around at what they had there, I didn't see anything impressive enough to fly the ocean. Maybe it was a big airship the Buggers could shoot down.

I admit I was nervous. I believe I still had some pressure in my head, and an overwhelming desire to lay down. We climbed in a lorry. I remember that because English lorries with hard wooden seats always rode smooth as a brick. It rode so hard, I could feel my brains banging against my skull. We unloaded alongside an airplane. Another surprise, here's one that I knew. It was from Hollywood. Now how about that? Of all the airplanes in the world, they're going to put me on the only one I know. I know this one by the movies. Shirley Temple sang, "on the good ship lollipop," while the cute little doll ran up and down the aisle. The plane looked fine, standing, wings spread, chin in the air. Of course at the time I didn't know anything about planes, or that this one was soon to be famous for delivering paratroops and gliders, a Douglas DC-3.

Right now my only thoughts were of the days and days it took for the freighter we came over on to cross over, and the width of the water of the Atlantic, with the mountainous waves of the storm that

179

could toss a ten-thousand-ton ship around like a floating soap bar. That was the Atlantic, and this was a skinny little plane, even with its two engines. It reminded me of a great-looking, slick pussy cat about to try and cross a boulevard, a wide boulevard. And again I thought, *How can I get out of this without seeming to scratch and cluck, giving me away as a chicken?* Sure, it's easy for anyone reading this to think, *What's the big deal?* You know I made it. But at the time, I damn sure didn't.

Here they're feeding me the same bullshit, like jumping off the troopship again, swimming to a Carley float, taking care not to be run over by the officers' lifeboats. How come? I've heard even the German prisoners are sent over to Canada by ship. What are they doing, cutting down on the loss of ships by using planes? And so on, and so on. Mentally I'm bitching again. How's it going to get me out of this? Until I hear, "All right, you guys, stop mooning about. Get up in the plane. You can wear the liner of the helmet and put the steel part in your lap. That's for all you guys that are going to throw up."

Hey now! Well, that should pass the time. Oh well, it's good-bye, Mother, time again. My Dragon is pulling out the hairs one by one.

I couldn't believe the seat I was to sit in; it was just a dent in a strip of aluminum with a lap belt strap, like what you tied your school books with as a kid. You know, usually Dad's worn out old belt. Looking at the strap, and the guy next to me strapping up also, I just said for no reason, "How do you think they got these planes over here, by flying? I can't believe they're going to get us home in this."

"Nah!" he said, "I heard we're only flying up to Scotland. These small planes stay here. They have bigger planes up there for flying around the ocean."

Oh now! The breath of life again. Hell, I feel a lot better now. Unfortunately I missed the inference of the word "around" in what he said. It never occurred to me that they didn't fly straight across, and this would cause me some gray hairs later, when I thought the Dragon was about to dump me in the sea.

The Shirley Temple plane flew us up to Scotland. And wasn't that a gas, and a great upchuck for some? I heard later the air over this coast of England, and the English Channel, is the roughest in the world. I had never been in a plane before, much less been off the ground, and the trip to Scotland had been one of constant dipping and climbing, shuddering and noise. The "bench" seats all facing inward gave us only an occasional glimpse out of one of the tiny, dirty windows, leaving me wondering if we were still right-side-up. The best I was able to do was hold on to the helmet in my lap. Even though I hadn't gotten sick, I was sure thinking of it, wondering if I could ever last for a long trip like one over the ocean, because I had gotten a little queasy a couple of times. Since then, no matter where I have flown, I've never known the air to be more turbulent. And now, with my legs still wobbly and my eyes trying to focus, my confidence was renewed.

As we got off the airplane, we were taken to a very big plane, a Rolls Royce in comparison. It wasn't only big; it wasn't skinny. It was stout, or I guess the word is wide, and with four big motors yet! Wow! Along the side of this big, beautiful new plane it said: U.S. Army Air Force Transportation, or I can't remember the exact wording, but it was something like that, because I thought, *Now you're talkin'*. I never knew they had such things. And if anything could make it, this baby sure looked right for the job.

I can even feel that old confidence in me as I write this. Because up until then, I've got to admit I was thinking hard of some way to get out of this. Oh, yes, yes, yes. I might have been a little nutty at that point, but not suicidal, a sort of *get me out of here* feeling.

The next *Alice in Wonderland* bit was an apparently very happy guy (the pilot) explaining how we were all going to be "short snorters" and to get a dollar bill signed by the crew who flew you across to prove it. He added, "You'll want to save these souvenirs, because not many guys have them." *Oh yeah*, I thought, *because maybe not too many have made it!*

You have to understand my feelings of trepidation, because very few people ever flew at all back then, never mind the ocean! But hell now, let's go!

I got aboard, found a window and snuggled up to it. I still couldn't get my mind to focus right, but at least now I could sit down out of the way in a nice padded chair where I could see the huge wing and those big, powerful motors do their dance. And after, it would seem, they'd shaken off enough dust and were panting to be unleashed, the power of them vibrated through the entire plane. "Buckle up," the nurse explained as she gave me a nice blanket to cover and comfort me.

Looking out the window I saw we were beginning to move. Bumping and shaking and, suddenly, like magic, with a movement almost surreal, the serene, quiet pleasure of our becoming airborne. Hey now! Isn't that a line? "Almost surreal, serene movement we became airborne." It was lovely, but it isn't me. It's my mind and this pencil; we're on a roll. Well, to get back . . . Look at me! I'm flying! My fear dropped away. I guess since I've never fallen from the sky, I can't relate to it. But maybe my word "queasy" would still fit.

As I stare out my window, I see a small dot, like a bug, on the window. It's swinging from side to side and growing larger by the second. There's another above and beside it. They're planes, Royal planes. As they turn, I see the bull's eyes on the wings. Royal British aircraft playing with us, giving us a Royal send-off and protection from any possible beloved black crosses. By God—and I say this reverently—there will never be any black crosses flying over my home. Or my people! We'll see to that.

It's true! I made it! I'm going home, flying. Flying home to see my mom and dad again. And a visit to my, as promised, undisturbed room, where I can be as snug as a bug in a rug . . . Oh! I'm laying back in the chair. It's so comforting, mentally and physically. If only this bundle of blanket in my lap was that of the girl from Jefferson, Indiana. I embraced it, nuzzled it, as I thought of her. Can't think of her name. Funny, she sure turned me on, but I can't . . . Now the rock-solid look of the plane and the hum of engines filled my mind. I'm going to go to sleep; hope it's the girl this time, not the Dragons. Wow! That's great! It's the girl. She's here in my lap. How did? What? Who cares? Her hands are like claws, pulling at me, teeth biting my ear. How come? Now we're all packed in the back of her dad's car, two boys and two girls. Her dad is taking us to some fair. I hope it's a long trip. Her dad is a coal miner and looks as tough as a chiseled-out piece of the stuff he digs. First time I met him, I ruled out ever throwing a punch in his direction; that would be tantamount to stepping in front of a train! *Be good, David! Be good.* Now Jessy—was it Jessy or Josie? Who cares?—she's wormed her fluffy bosom up to cut off my breath. She's chewing on my ear. I'm busy working away with my questing hand under that voluminous dress, directing my fingers. My fingers don't need no directing; my fingers have no nose, but they sure "knows" the right direction! They're surreptitiously working their way up the unguarded, trembling inner thigh of her right leg, heading ever upward. Hey! I'll be in like a tall dog! Whoooee! Just got up over the top of the stocking. Stop panting! Who's panting. Oh, lordy, hold still, honey; don't wiggle. Your dad will bust my head. Uh-oh, I hear yelling. Sounds like the shit's hit the fan. Sounds like I'm in for it, as well I should be for dreaming of the girl like this. Sure, I know I'm dreaming. My mind needs protection from that nightmare of having the Dragons chase me down a torn-up path strewn with the mangled parts of men, and more coming down by parachute, with the boys in them upside down, even piled in a heap. What? Of course I know that's impossible, but that's why I'd rather dream something impossibly good than impossibly bad. I've been down that bad path before. So you can't blame me for wanting the pleasure of a girl's company. *Relax, man. Finish the dream, David. Stay with it.* Now what's it to be? Her dad tearing off my head, or just using his iron hand to crush my scrotum? Her hugging arms strangling me, or my suffocating under the dress?

My eyes snap open. Oh, hell, I've been dreaming! There's a hubbub in the cabin. What's going on? Funny, the plane feels like I'm on an elevator, descending. I can feel myself going down. Even slowing down. I turned to my window to see if I could see the ocean. I pulled back, startled. Christ! It was almost like getting a punch in the face. Now I see what the yelling is about. One of the motors, the outboard motor, is belching black greasy smoke, just like the time of the tanks, that terrible day with the Shermans. I can see it now. The sight leaps into my eyes. Not that again! Soaring columns of flame and smoke, flashing, exploding smoke and blasts, cutting down even the crew guys who had managed to escape their confines. Men running for their lives! Oh, hell! I knew it was too good to be true. I'm not mad. Hell, why be mad? I always knew home was just a dream. Sure. And then again, you know, maybe I'm still in my hospital bed dreaming. No, no, this is real; those Dragons were only playing with me, and now they've pulled the plug. I wonder if we could make it on three engines, or maybe it will burn off that end of the wing. Could we still make it?

My enlisting was my wanting to fight, and I damn sure got it. But the laugh of it all is, the ones I fought never got to tag me, but my own people did. And now they're going to finish it off. Oh well, now anyway, cuddled in that big chair, I did get to enjoy a great dream. Now, of course, there will be no returning hero, no girl, no parents, just fish, because the fish will get their dinner tonight.

A hand is shaking me. It's the nurse saying, "Save your tears, Mr Lawrie. We're about to land."

What? Tears? Me? Hell, I was half asleep again! Can't I get awake? Waddayah trying to do, girly, console me? And I don't cry. And I also know this plane's got wheels, wheels that are no good for the middle of the ocean! I had unbuckled myself, pushing aside and dumping the blanket that I had thought was my girl. My face! Holy hell, it's wet! I really must have been in tears. What's happened to me?

Then, before my bewildered eyes, a Quonset hut flashed by under the wing. Up here? A flying Quonset hut? Of course not! Am I still dreaming? Then my knees buckled as the wheels hit the ground. I let my hands and knees enjoy the rumbling, bumping ride as the plane's wheels rolled along on solid ground, giving life to my body yet again . . . yet again.

Iceland. Beautiful Iceland. I only say that because it saved my life. Because this place has got to be the most miserable, God-forsaken land ever, even outdoing Africa. Rectum of the world! Nothing but mud and rocks as far as I could see. There were shacks and Quonset huts serving as a terminal, and huge stacks of wooden boxes filled with apples. Seems a ship loaded with apples was torpedoed and towed in here to salvage the cargo. Welcome to Iceland, mates, and have an apple if you please.

Later I met, I would think, the youngest soldier I had ever seen. I had to start up a conversation with him. I said, "I thought only the navy took sixteen year olds." He just gave me a laughing look; it was in his eyes. He was an air gunner, and proud of it. After a lot of practice in some desert somewhere, he was on a flight to England and they had plane trouble too. He was in the Army Air Corps, and he and his buddies couldn't wait to get those black crosses in their sights.

I didn't put him down. I wouldn't waste my time putting down any young person. We all make that climb, sometimes a very tough climb, to reach the pinnacle, to achieve manhood or womanhood, to reach our level of competence. But as we do, unknowingly we reach our own peaks, and the other side of that mountain is a slow but sure "down." And if you live long enough, you'll reach the valley of everlasting groans in your eighties and nineties. Everything in your body will seem to get stiff, except (pardon me) your penis. Then, eventually, the worst: dying in bed! As I said before, I want o die chasing girls, shot by a jealous young man. Oh, there I go again, rambling away. Anyway, as long as you're young, who knows anything about getting old, or even thinks of it? We all, in time, must shed our virgin minds. Some do it easily, and others must learn, well, as you know, the hard way. I wished him luck. And I really meant it. Him and all the happy, rambunctious, young and innocent gunners to be. Because I knew—I'd seen with my own eyes—many of their planes go down. Again, it's our cost, a bitter cost. Yet we will prevail, making the cost of freedom less in the future. No, I didn't give him my lecture. I just wobbled around, killing time till I was put on another plane to be flown to Greenland.

Heading for Greenland I couldn't relax or let my eyes close, thinking, *Why did they do this to me? This is not a normal way to travel. People in the future will never do this voluntarily.* As soon as we take off, it seems my testicles start hugging each other. The calming balm is that we're getting so close to the end of my journey. What could possibly happen next? I felt like the story of the Dragon slayer after a tough bout with the beast, on his way home, being assailed by the fickle fingers of fate. Yet muddling through. You may think my mind has been captured by the mythical Dragons I had come to believe in, and that it's all silly, but how silly are guys who put their faith in gods, beads or prayers? Remember on the beach, when the tanks were closing on me and I prayed, no, I demanded help from whatever Dragon it was I was under? And *Wham!*, I got a battleship! Unbelievable. A battleship to blow them beloved bastards away, and leave me to dancing, howling in triumph! What other God could you ask to do that? I know, you think I've crossed the line. No one can criticize any God for failing. But when it's *my* butt in the fire, and I've seen too many failed prayers, crumpled, laying face down, my mythical God can be as good as your mythical one.

My mind working with my pencil is fantastic, almost like a computer with an endless memory. You must remember, I've promised to tell the truth, as I've spent a lifetime trying to do. I can't be a hypocrite and deny my feelings. It may at times raise hackles in some people, even though I try not to, but after all, I'm the guy that was put to the test!

Landing at Greenland was great even though it was still far north, had a name similar to Iceland, and looked as bleak. But it was altogether different. Here was a real airport full of people doing their jobs. Even the Red Cross guys who came aboard, walking up the aisles like candy hawkers on trains selling box lunches for five dollars each, no doubt they hadn't been told the plane they were on was an extra one, put together in Iceland, replacing the one carrying hospital cases. And of course, none of us had any money. Even so, they still wouldn't give us any on the "arm" (credit), and subsequently they were booed off the plane. When I told my father this part, he had a fit. He worked for the Elco boat company in New Jersey building those wooden torpedo boats that were sent to the Pacific to sink Jap ships. He said that every week when the men were paid they donated a lot more money to the Red Cross than would buy a few lunches for the boys.

Well, that was the worst that happened on the last legs of the trip. From Greenland we flew to LaGuardia, or someplace on Long Island, and of course Brooklyn is on Long Island, so I'm home! I made it! My sojourn started with a subway ride from Brooklyn, and if my endless luck holds, can end with a subway ride back to Brooklyn.

Return

Getting off the plane, I felt like someone returning to earth. I was enthralled, truly. I could easily feel the rapture of any astronaut returning to earth after a long, long journey through endless obstacles to his life. Here it was, a life of normalcy, a life I had taken for granted, the life I had been born into. It was like stepping through a door that I had assumed had been closed forever, closed forever on my boyish memories. Of course it was only the door of the plane, but I could see the world of peace as I stepped out onto the platform carried by a truck, a little truck that mounted a stairway, not a 50-cal, and observed people walking about bare headed, not a helmet in sight. No one carrying the ever-present, inarguable badge of the soldier, his rifle, slung or hung on his shoulder or hand. No one staring at the sky because it's blue and friendly. There's not a weapon in sight. Guys bustled about in like summer jeans, not uniforms. But the greatest, the greatest—look over there, what all of us fought for! A big, beautiful American flag. What could possibly cost more than that, that symbol of freedom? Causing acid in the tyrant's eye. Wave, baby, wave. Here it was, the life I had lived so casually before I had enlisted. The real world, not the endlessly uptight madhouse I had found myself in doing my duty in the army. Here were my people, people working to live, to build, to manufacture, not to kill. How can anyone put down the idea of a democracy?

Now I truly felt I was in the hometown locker room. Everyone, everyone was on my side. What a feeling. Not to worry, we're with you. We're the greatest! So are you.

I was ecstatic, blood rushing through my veins. I made it! Brooklyn to Brooklyn in WWII. It wasn't very long; it was condensed to a purpose, changing a boy to a man. No, not a man, a soldier. I hereby claim the title: soldier. I earned it, because that's all it took, effort, blood, brains, and a little skin. Brooklyn to Brooklyn in World War II. It seemed forever, but only took exactly eight hundred days. Eight hundred days of mine.

Sure, LaGuardia is in Queens, but the same subway that took me to Grand Central Station for a nickel to join the army also runs in Queens and would for another nickel have taken me home to Brooklyn. If only for a visit. But they wouldn't let me go. I couldn't have done anything anyway.

When I went overseas I was 185 pounds, and I remember when my sister Helen visited me in the hospital later, she remarked how my chart showed I was down to 138. Eventually the Veterans Administration was formed and I was given my Honorable Medical Discharge,

100 percent service connected to the VA, where now for some sixty years I've been at various times worked on by the surgeons for an eye, a leg, a stomach, some fractured bones in my spine, getting all those uncountable free operations. Oh yeah!

Something else I got for "free" with operations was the pleasant visits to La La Land via the anesthesia used. I believe the total count, can't swear, but it's close, comes to fifteen; that's fifteen operations, including the biggest ever, the quadruple bypass. But that was two weeks in intensive care, ten days of unconsciousness, with no surreal dreams. All I remember of that was seeing the clock on the wall at the foot of my bed, and daylight flashing by, with a lot of sympathetic heads peering at mine. But of course that was recent (2001). Since then I have had two more operations on both my eyes (2005), but they don't count, because anesthesia can't be used, so no induced dream. On an eye operation, for some reason, you must remain awake to answer questions while they work on your eyes, so all you can do is just relax, grit your teeth and try not to howl.

Now, about my trips to La La Land. Of course these ethereal trips can't be regarded as the truth, but only insofar as I perceived them. They are brought on and experienced by a lack of consciousness. And the gist of it should be familiar to readers of this travail, as they follow my aforementioned exactly eight hundred "daze" of service to my country. And my country, in turn, as promised, and I'm proud to say, never neglected its sixty years of service to me. As a disabled (70 percent) combat veteran, never a charge for medical care or medicine. And that's with the best of care. I give accolades to the Veterans Administration for keeping me alive. Plus a monthly stipend—shall we say, a bonus for good work.

I was discharged into the veterans care at 100 percent service connected, but this has now been reduced over the years to 70 percent, as I was able to go to work. Still the guarantee, including any and all medical care. But in the early days of veteran care, we were shunted around to various commandeered hospitals until the Veterans Administration could build its own. Also, the art of operating on so many cases, in time, led to better techniques, as in mine. As an example, whenever they were coming to get me to push me to the operating room, it always involved the effort on my part, as they say today, to look cool despite the turmoil inside my guts—the fake laughing and jokes as I felt the relentless pushing , pushing of the gurney taking me to my possible demise. Unarmed as usual, all I could do as we went was to occupy my weary mind with my looking at the ceiling, keep faking the grin as they tie me down. Christ! How many times must I prove that I'm a man! Although I feel like a man with lessening grit. Then, as always, I thought of the Dragon card; you know, like the battleship bit. *Do it again, you hairy, flaming monster. Dim me out. Ease me through one of these endless trips to the freezer to be cut up.* Now, remember, I'm telling you things so that when your turn comes (if you live long enough) you won't feel so bad doing it. I talked to myself, that is, I talked to my mentor, my Dragon, and to put off the idea of a direct plea, I deliberately thought, *Oh no, he couldn't do anything about that! I'm sure all them Dragons are all back in Europe enjoying the feast. Normandy had been invaded.* But of course they were never back in Europe; they were, as always, only in my mind. But then, like a whisper, a feeling something's coming, it comes—the slightest rustling in my ear, or is it in my head? How does a fiery, rasping tongue manage to whisper? I hear, like a hoarse murmur, *howzzat! hey! howzzat!* What? What? What's zzat?

Looking at my prone body in the bed, wondering, *Howzzat? What was that?* And damned, like a vision, as I lay in the bed bleary-eyed, behold! Here comes a beautiful nurse. Now, you must remember, when you're still a little goopy from previous shots, the sight of a nurse is always beautiful; then it would seem my Dragon's coming to my rescue, having produced another miracle! Or so it seems. She said with lilting voice, "Hi, Mr. Lawrie, ready to go? Got something new for you. The doctors have developed what they call a 'happy shot.'"

The doctors made a happy shot? Is that what was meant when I blearily heard that hoarse whisper, *howzzat*? Guys asked for ease to the trip, so they put together this shot to help you relax while they get you ready. And she just popped it in my arm. This was simply a shot in the arm of some carefree juice, so that by the time the they came to get me, I was really carefree. Whoopee! Bless all you Dragons. Or your imaginary presence.

As I lay there wondering what started me fearing or praying

hopefully to Dragons, eyes closed, I can see it now, the greatest, most powerful "spear" of combat men I had ever seen—twenty-four brand new Sherman tanks tearing up the earth, tracks flinging clods of earth in their haste to get at the puny prey. Going in behind my company, Company A, backed up by tank destroyers was truly the most fear-not time of my life. What support! We'll tear them apart! If the Germans haven't run, we'll make them wish they had.

But then as I watch, dumbfounded, the great dream is ripped apart. It's not them, it's us! We're being blown and torn apart! Get out of the way; the men are running at us. The tanks fleeing will run us over! Look, it's not from the enemy, it's Dragons! Monster Dragons! Oh, damn them to hell! There's nothing visible to shoot at. My rounds bounce off them!

Well, they're going to fix my stomach. They claim they can put me back together. I quote what I was told by one Surgeon: "Yes sir, son, we'll give you a stomach you can eat barbed wire with!" Oh yeah!

Remember, I ain't dead yet! Damn near it, but I'm still a fighter. And never mind the barbed wire. I'll settle for a banana!

And now for La La Land. Picture me as I lay on a gurney being slowly wheeled down a long hall. I've been taken from my bed after getting what they call a "happy shot." My eyes are following the tile lines in the ceiling and the fluorescent lights as they go by. Now I can tell we're entering the operating room; these rooms always seem to be kept cool or even cold. And I hear laughter; people in these rooms always seem to have the need for laughter. Maybe it's because they're not the ones lying still, strapped down, waiting to be excised in some manner. But who cares? The happy shot is really working. If they decided to throw me out a window, I wouldn't care.

Now, as I lay here amid all the burbling talk, my mind begins to drift. I heard the word "soldier." That's got to refer to me. I'm the only soldier in this room. I made it! All the worry I had that I could never measure up was blown away in all the violent action. You bet I made it! But Dad, I also became a very mean and nasty bastard. Soldier isn't necessarily a shining word. But I'm still proud to be one.

Now just a word to the reader. Remember, I'm writing about my mind. I'm not writing to impress you or looking for praise or sympathy. My goal is to pass on to some future young man that may have to walk where I have just walked, to help preserve his life. To love peace and liberty, we must always be ready to show our teeth, might and muscle, to assail any enemy with a professionally trained armed force, a force that can be USED! The greatest weapons in the world are worthless if you haven't got the determination to use them! Our rules should be to declare our intent, then with certainty move to destroy anyone or anything that threatens our women and children, or our way of life that was intended to comfort them. Then, if we must fight, fight like hell! And when you do hit them, hit them hard. Others will take note and not be so quick threaten us.

I have heard General Patton was once told that if you do that, people will hate you. He retorted: "I don't care how much they hate me, as long as they fear me."

Now, me, David (2007), the tough and, at times, maniacal soldier, unbelievably dying like a wilting snowman in bed! I have a crazy wish, a wish to be back with all the guys, my buddies, guys who were scared tough, not just to fight, but to take it as well.

As were we all.

What else can I say? God has let me come home. In spite of all of my irreverences, I can still hold up my battered body and say, "It was a breeze! Oh yeah! . . ."